Combination
C O O K E R Y
à la carte

Combination
C O O K E R Y

CAROLINE STEVENS AND DEBORAH ROBB

Boxtree

First published in Great Britain in 1989 by Boxtree Limited

No part of this book may be reproduced in any form without prior permission from the
publisher

Copyright © 1989 Grub Street, London
Text copyright © Caroline Stevens and Deborah Robb
Design copyright © Grub Street, London
Photographs by Tim Imrie
Illustrations by Toula Antonakos
Edited by Jenni Fleetwood

Food prepared and styled for photography by Caroline Stevens and Deborah Robb

Typeset by Chapterhouse, The Cloisters, Formby
Printed and bound in Great Britain by Maclehose and Partners, Portsmouth for
Boxtree Limited, 36 Tavistock Street, London WC2E 7PB

British Library Cataloguing in Publication Data
Stevens, Caroline
    Combination cookery à la carte
    1. Food: Dishes prepared using combination ovens —
    Recipes
    I. Title   II. Robb, Deborah
    641.5'88

    ISBN 1-85283-274-6

FRONT JACKET PHOTOGRAPH:
Chicken amaretto (page 60); Prawn mousselines (page 30); Brandy snap horns with
raspberry sauce (page 100).

BACK JACKET PHOTOGRAPH:
Vegetable terrine with pimiento purée (page 26); Chicken with roquefort in filo pastry
(page 61); Celery au gratin (page 74); Grape and almond tart (page 97).

CONTENTS

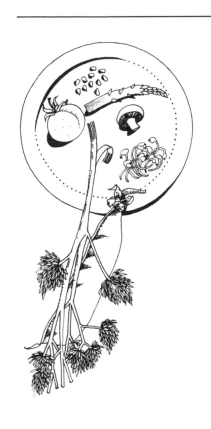

We would like to dedicate this to our families and friends who have given us their support while we have been writing this book. Especially to Barbara, Sally, Juliette, Tina, Libby and Lynette who have had our children to play when we needed time to work, and to Fran who helped us with the typing. Our thanks also go to the staff of the Kitchen Design Centre, Colchester where the Contemporary Cookery School is based and to manufacturers of combination ovens who have assisted us, particularly Sharp, Panasonic and Bosch.

FOREWORD

Successful entertaining has never been simpler. The combination oven not only cooks to perfection – preserving textures and flavours with consistent reliability; conserving colours and nutrients – it also crisps and browns to produce dishes that look as good as they taste. Best of all, it grants a busy host the one gift valued above all else: time. Time to greet guests, time to unwind in good company, time for the finishing touches that turn a simple meal into a memorable event.

Entertaining is not just a shared meal; it is an occasion. Planning menus, selecting wines and choosing convivial and stimulating company can be almost as satisfying as the event itself.

Equally, impromptu parties can be enormous fun, so be rash occasionally and invite friends on the spur of the moment. Make sure you have a ready supply of wine and other drinks so that your guests can sit around the kitchen table and chat to you while you are cooking. This shouldn't take long with your combination oven and your guests will be amazed at the speed with which you can produce a gourmet meal.

Whether the party is planned or spontaneous, you will find recipes here to fit the bill, from the extravagant to the frugal. Where possible we have taken shortcuts to keep preparation time to the minimum while still producing impressive, mouthwatering dishes which are a delight to look at, smell and especially taste.

This book contains a collection of many of our favourite recipes for entertaining, many of which have happy associations and conjure up marvellous memories. We hope they will do the same for you.

CAROLINE STEVENS AND DEBORAH ROBB

INTRODUCTION

WHAT IS A COMBINATION OVEN?

The combination oven gives the choice of three or more cooking systems:

1. Microwave
2. Conventional oven, possibly convection or fan-assisted
3. Combination, i.e. Microwave and oven simultaneously

Many combination ovens also have a grill which may be used on its own or in some instances combined with the microwave.

In this book we have used the different systems to achieve the best results in each recipe. We hope that when you have cooked your way through the book you will not only have discovered some delicious new recipes but will also have a better understanding of how your combination oven works.

THE SYSTEMS EXPLAINED

THE MICROWAVE SYSTEM

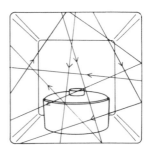

Microwave

Microwaves are high frequency waves similar to radio and television waves. They are attracted to the moisture in food causing the molecules to vibrate. This creates friction, which in turn produces heat to cook the food quickly and efficiently. Try rubbing your hands together and you will see how quickly friction creates heat.

Electrical energy enters the oven via the magnetron which converts it into microwaves. Once released, these are continuously reflected off the metal walls of the oven, which also contains them safely within the cavity.

Microwaves travel in straight lines in a set pattern and for that reason your combination oven will either have a turntable or stirrer to ensure even cooking of food. The turntable will mechanically turn the food around whereas the stirrer (also referred to as the wave guide or delta wave revolving antenna) causes the microwaves to enter the oven in a random pattern. Individually both methods will give you even cooking of food, although some ovens will have both.

Microwaves are absorbed by the food they heat, so the oven remains cool. Microwaves penetrate the food to a depth of 3.5 cm (1½ inches) producing heat instantly. The heat then spreads by conduction and for this reason standing times are important when the microwave system is used on its own.

Although they pass unhindered through materials such as glass, china and certain plastics, microwaves are reflected by metal. For further information see **Cooking Utensils** on page 11.

The microwave system is particularly good for defrosting, reheating, melting, poaching, boiling and simmering.

THE OVEN SYSTEM

Conventional oven

This is thermostatically controlled and can be used as any other oven. Many models, even some with a turntable, will allow you to cook on two levels. Because this system is like a traditional oven, the oven will become hot and so any splashes or spills will be baked on. Regular cleaning is thus essential. Some models have special easy-clean finishes or cleaning programmes. There are three different ways of heating the oven:

1. CONVENTIONAL

This is by heating elements in the top and bottom of your oven. They are usually hidden, so may not be apparent.

2. FAN

This may be called turbo or convection or something similar depending on the manufacturer. The heating elements surround the fan which is usually at the back of the oven. This type of oven heats up very quickly and will require little preheating.

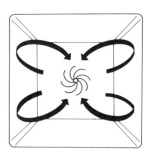

Fan oven

3. FAN ASSISTED

This method uses conventional heating elements with the addition of a fan to boost the circulation of heat.

N.B. WHERE THE TERM CONVENTIONAL OVEN IS USED IN THIS BOOK IT REFERS TO ANY OF THE ABOVE.

All cooking utensils suitable for a traditional oven may be used for the conventional system. For further information see **Cooking Utensils** on page 11. The oven system is particularly good for cooking small items which need rapid browning and crisping.

Fan assisted oven

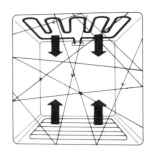

Conventional combination oven

Fan combination oven

Fan assisted combination oven

THE COMBINATION SYSTEM

This may be called Combi, High speed, Dual, Multifunction or similar according to the manufacturer. This is where the oven and microwave operate simultaneously. The conventional heat browns and crisps while the microwave speeds up the cooking time. This gives traditional browning with a faster cooking time.

In many cases combination cooking gives much better results than cooking in a conventional oven. You gain the best characteristics of microwave cooking – speed, light texture of cakes, bright vegetable colour and minimum loss of nutrients – together with the benefits of conventional cooking: browning, crisping and flavour.

The combination system is particularly beneficial for recipes that would normally need more than 25 minutes to cook.

Utensils used must be able to withstand heat and microwaves. Some manufacturers permit the use of metal containers. We have had some very good results using metal in some ovens but it is important to check with your manufacturer before using metal. For further information see **Cooking Utensils** on page 11.

TECHNIQUES FOR COMBINATION COOKING

TURNING FOOD AND STIRRING. We have found it beneficial to turn meat and poultry halfway through the cooking period to give even cooking. In some ovens it is advisable to turn the dish occasionally. Stirring is suggested in some recipes particularly where the microwave is used on its own.

STANDING TIMES. These are important where the microwave is used on its own, but not so important where the combination system is used. Foods such as meats will carve more easily if left to rest after cooking for 10 minutes to firm up. Cakes should be left for at least 5 minutes in the dish in which they were cooked before turning out. Where standing times are essential, they will be given in the recipe.

COVERING. In all cooking methods covering is necessary where you wish to retain moisture and speed up cooking times. Where the microwave only is used this can be done with a suitable lid, dinner plate or microwave film. When the appliance is used as a conventional oven metal lids or foil may be used but for combination cooking materials used must generally be both heatproof and suitable for the microwave. See **Cooking Utensils** on page 11.

PREHEATING. We have found the best results are achieved by putting food into a hot oven. Some manufacturers disagree, so be guided by your handbook. Preheating times vary tremendously between different ovens and can be as little as 2 minutes to as much as 20 minutes. Use only conventional energy to preheat the oven. Microwaves may only be introduced if there is food in the oven. It is perfectly acceptable to use the preheating period to microwave onions, sauces etc but remember that the oven will be getting hot, so use appropriate cookware.

Stirring

*Stir from the outside
of the dish to the inside in order
to distribute heat.*

Turning

*Turn foods occasionally to
ensure even cooking.*

Covering

*Cover roasts with a tent of
foil whilst standing.*

COOKING UTENSILS

MICROWAVE		CONVENTIONAL COOKING		COMBINATION COOKING
Suitable	*Unsuitable*	*Suitable*	*Unsuitable*	Be guided by what your manufacturer's instruction book says. Some manufacturers of combination ovens allow the use of certain metal containers but do check with your handbook. The following dishes are suitable for all models.
glass	lead crystal	oven-proof	plastic	
glazed ceramic	unglazed	glass eg: pyrex	Tupperware	
china	earthenware	oven-proof	plastic film	
rigid plastic	Tupperware	ceramics	lead crystal	
boiling bags	melamine	metal baking		
roasting bags	metal dishes of	tins and trays		
paper	any type,	cast iron		
microwave	including foil	casserole		
suitable plastic	containers and	dishes		
film	dishes	heat resistant		*Suitable* — *Unsuitable*
	decorated with	plastic		ovenproof — plastic
	gold or silver	earthenware		glass — paper
	trim			heat resistant — metal
				plastic — casseroles with
				ovenproof — lids
				ceramics

Ovenproof glass, ceramic, or heat resistant plastic containers have been used in all the recipes tested for this book.

HOW TO ADAPT THE RECIPES FOR YOUR OVEN

This book includes recipes which are suitable for microwave alone, oven alone or combination cooking, which is when the microwave and oven operate simultaneously. Each recipe specifies the method to be used.

MICROWAVE
Where microwave alone is used we refer to HIGH, MEDIUM and LOW power settings; this corresponds as follows:

HIGH   600 Watts   MEDIUM   300 Watts   LOW   180 Watts

If your oven does not correspond exactly choose the closest power level and adjust the timing accordingly, i.e. a higher output will need less cooking time and a lower output will need more cooking time.

OVEN
Where the oven is used alone, this includes fan and fan-assisted systems, depending on your particular Combination oven. Recipes will clearly state that only conventional heat should be used. Preheating times will vary. All oven temperatures are given only in degrees Centigrade, since this is how combination ovens are graduated.

COMBINATION (oven and microwave working simultaneously)
Where the combination system is used in recipes we give an oven temperature followed by a microwave power level. *After preheating* these should be set to operate together, e.g. 200°C with LOW microwave for 20 minutes.

Where an oven has preset combination cooking, e.g. High speed, Dual, Combi etc, the manufacturer has already chosen the programme for you and you may not be able to adjust the microwave power to correspond exactly with our recipes. In testing recipes on various models we have found that quite a wide variation of microwave output achieves similar results. The following chart will act as a guide.

MAKE OF OVEN	HIGH	MEDIUM	LOW
AEG Micromat ex Duo **3214L/3214Z**	4 (600W)	3 (360W)	2 (180W)
Bejam BM801	high speed + extra time	high speed	high speed + less time
Belling 333	high	medium	low
Belling 343	high speed + extra time	high speed	high speed + less time
Bosch **Multimicro HBE 6920** **HBE 6900**	 1 (600W) 1 (600W)	 2 (360W) 2 (360W)	 3 (180W) 3 (180W)
Bosch **Multimicro 2 HBE 6800** **HBE 6820**	 4 (600W) 4 (600W)	 3 (360W) 3 (360W)	 2 (180W) 2 (180W)
Bosch HMG 2000 **HMG 2200**	600W	180W + extra time	180W
Bosch HMG 2010 **HMG 2210**	4 (600W) 4 (600W)	3 (360W) 3 (360W)	2 (180W) 2 (180)
Bosch HMG 8200/8220 **HMG 8400/8420**	600 600	360 360	180 180
Brother 2000	high	medium	low
Brother 2100	high speed + extra time	high speed	high speed + less time
Brother MF 2200	high speed + extra time	high speed	high speed + less time
Brother MF 2150	high speed + extra time	high speed	high speed + less time
Brother MF 3200	high speed + extra time	high speed	high speed + less time
Brother MF 1200	high speed + extra time	high speed	high speed + less time
Creda **MW Circulair 48208** **48216** **Concept MW Circulair 48312**	C7 or 8	C6, C5 or C2	C4 or C3
Fagor MW 2100 UK	combination setting + extra time	combination setting + extra time	combination setting

MAKE OF OVEN	HIGH	MEDIUM	LOW
Gaggenau 836/837	50%	25%	defrost
Hot Point 6680	600	180 + extra time	180
Miele M700 **(Eire only)**	600	300	150
Neff 6180	600	180 + extra time	180
6185	600	180 + extra time	180
Neff 6190	4	3	2
6195	4	3	2
Neff 1031 MW3	high	medium	low
Neff 7170/7175	600	300	180
Panasonic NE 972	2 + extra time	2	3
Panasonic NN 8807/8857	2 or 8 + extra time	2 or 5	3 or 4
Panasonic NE 992/993	2 + extra time	2	3
Panasonic NN 8507/8557	2 or 8 + extra time	2 or 5	3 or 4
Samsung RE 990CT	high	medium	medium low
RE 995CG	high	medium	medium low
Scholtes F2860	5	3 or 2	2 or 1
F2865	5	3 or 2	2 or 1
Sharp 8170	high (100%)	medium (50%)	medium low (30%)
8270	high (100%)	medium (50%)	medium low (30%)
8480	high (100%)	medium (50%)	medium low (30%)
8680	high (100%)	medium (50%)	medium low (30%)
8880	high (100%)	medium (50%)	medium low (30%)
Siemens HF 4200	600	180 + extra time	180
HF 4202	600	180 + extra time	180
Siemens HB 8704	1	2	3
Siemens HF 6504	4	3	2
HF 6502	4	3	2
Siemens HF 4300	4	3	2
HF 4302			
Siemens HB 7500			
HB 7502	1	2	3
Siemens HF 72000/72020	600	360	180
HF 74040/74020	600	360	180
Toshiba ER 9610	high	med–med low	med low–low
ER 9630	high	med–med low	med low–low
ER 9530	high	med–med low	med low–low

FAULT FINDING

FAULT	SUGGESTED REMEDIES
Food not brown enough	1. Check the oven was preheated before cooking. 2. Turn up the temperature next time. 3. Allow a little extra time at the end without the microwave.
Food not cooked but brown enough	1. Raise the microwave power. 2. Cook from a cold start. 3. Lower the oven temperature and cook for slightly longer.
Food brown enough but overcooked	1. Lower microwave power. 2. Shorten microwave time. 3. Add a little extra liquid where appropriate.
Bottom not cooked	1. If a flan, precook base for 5 minutes at 200°C, LOW power microwave before filling. 2. Preheat a metal tray (where manufacturers allow) or glass tray, with the oven and place the container on to this hot tray at the start of cooking.
Cracked cakes	1. Hollow out the top of the cake slightly before cooking.
Excess splashing (meats particularly)	1. Cook in a deeper dish. 2. Drain off any excess fat during cooking. 3. Lower the temperature. 4. Lower the power level.

ENTERTAINING

Entertaining is fun. Remember that your guests are not critics – even professional cooks love to go out and eat when they haven't had to plan the meal or do the shopping.

The secret of successful entertaining is good organisation – even with impromptu parties. The following guidelines will help you be the perfect host.

GUESTS

The idea is that all your guests should get on and stimulate each other into good conversation. You can play safe by inviting people who already know each other but it is always satisfying to introduce strangers and watch friendships blossom.

Our recipes cater for up to eight and most can easily be scaled up or down to suit your numbers. Six and eight are ideal numbers: beyond that there is the danger that the party will split and you may spend the evening trying to listen to two separate conversations.

There are those who divide guests into G.D.P.M. and B.D.P.M. The aim is to get yourself classified as G.D.P.M. – good dinner party material – that way you will never be short of an invitation!

MENU

Firstly check on the likes and dislikes of your guests so that you can plan a menu you know they will enjoy.

Start by choosing one course (it doesn't matter which), then plan your other courses to complement it, bearing in mind it is better to do a simple thing well than a complicated dish badly.

When choosing a menu bear in mind the following:

- Advance cooking: choose some recipes that can be prepared well in advance and frozen or stored so that there is no last minute panic.
- Temperature: it is a good idea to have at least one cold course. A cold starter is ideal because it can be set out before guests arrive. If every course is hot you will spend more time in the kitchen than with your guests.
- Colour and texture: you should aim to have contrasting colours and textures throughout the meal. Nothing is more unappetizing than an entire meal made up of soft textures and dull colours.
- Nutritional content: this often goes by the board when entertaining. No one wants to count calories when enjoying a good evening out; you can always diet the next day! However, so many people are trying to cut down on the amount of fat they eat that it is a good idea to avoid using cream and butter in everything. It is also important not to overface your guests with large quantities – you can always offer more.

DRINKS

You don't have to be an expert or a millionaire to choose wines these days. Most off-licenses and supermarkets will offer advice. Generally red wine goes with meat and game and white wine with white meat and fish but this rule does not always have to be followed. If you want to really go to town and impress, choose a different wine for each course, but this is not absolutely necessary.

Make sure that the wine is served at the right temperature and have plenty of mineral water and soft drinks available for drivers or thirsty guests.

If you don't want to play barman with the pre-dinner drinks it is a good idea to serve sparkling wine or champagne, or a simple cocktail which can be mixed in a jug.

If you have time prepare a canapé or two to make mouths water. After the meal petit fours, fresh coffee and liqueur or port will go down well.

PREPARATION

We find the following work plan helps to make a successful occasion. It is only a guide and need not be followed rigidly.

1. Plan the menu and wine.

2. Write the shopping list and ideally do the shopping at least the day before.
3. Make as many dishes in advance as possible.
4. Lay the table and tidy up the bits your guests will see!
5. Get your kitchen in order and prepare any ingredients for last-minute cooking. In this way you can be sure that you have all that is necessary.
6. Check that everything is as near to complete as you can make it without spoiling.
7. Pamper yourself in a warm bath and get ready.
8. Set out the nibbles, then sit down and have a quiet few minutes to collect your thoughts before your guests arrive.
9. Delegate someone to look after the drinks.
10. Do the last minute finishing off, serve, eat and enjoy. You deserve it!

A FINAL NOTE

By all means use your combination oven for the entire meal if you want to. We have done so on some occasions, but you will find your entertaining easier and more enjoyable if you use your combination oven in conjunction with the hob, or your ordinary oven. Select those dishes best suited for each appliance, perhaps keeping plates and food warm in your normal oven or making sauces on the hob while any last-minute cooking or rapid reheating is done in the combination oven. Above all remember that entertaining should be fun and if you enjoy it so will your guests.

CONVERSION CHART

WEIGHTS		LIQUID MEASURE		LINEAR MEASURE	
Metric	*Imperial*	*Metric*	*Imperial*	3 mm	⅛ in
25 g	1 oz	30 ml	1 fl oz	5 mm	¼ in
50 g	2 oz	60 ml	2 fl oz	1 cm	½ in
75 g	3 oz	90 ml	3 fl oz	2.5 cm	1 in
125 g	4 oz	120 ml	4 fl oz	5 cm	2 in
150 g	5 oz	150 ml	¼ pint (5 fl oz)	7.5 cm	3 in
175 g	6 oz	300 ml	½ pint (10 fl oz)	10 cm	4 in
200 g	7 oz	450 ml	¾ pint (15 fl oz)	13 cm	5 in
225 g	8 oz	600 ml	1 pint (20 fl oz)	15 cm	6 in
250 g	9 oz	1 litre	1¾ pint (35 fl oz)	18 cm	7 in
275 g	10 oz			20 cm	8 in
300 g	11 oz			23 cm	9 in
350 g	12 oz			25 cm	10 in
375 g	13 oz			28 cm	11 in
400 g	14 oz			30 cm	12 in
425 g	15 oz				
450 g	16 oz (1 lb)				
1 kg (i.e. 1000 g)	2¼ lb				

5 ml = 1 teaspoon (tsp)
15 ml = 1 tablespoon (tbsp)
As the above conversions are not exact, use either Metric or Imperial measures but do not mix the two.

SOUPS, STARTERS AND SNACKS

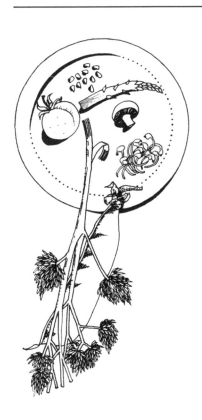

SOUPS AND STARTERS should be really tasty and attractive. Many people say that this is their favourite course and that they could eat a whole meal of starters. There are restaurants that specialize in serving just starters and desserts. Certainly all the recipes in this section fit the bill, and will really stimulate the appetite.

Some starters in this section are very light, such as the smoked salmon mousse and the vegetable terrine; others are more substantial and make perfect light meals or snacks; for example the smoked haddock and mushroom crackers.

Your combination oven will be invaluable in the preparation of soups, starters and snacks and whether you use merely the microwave, the oven or the combination method of cooking, any one of the delicious recipes that follow will get your dinner party off to a good start.

SOUFFLÉ TOPPED SOUP

SERVES 6

•

30 ml (2 tbsp) oil

3 cloves garlic, crushed

1 large onion, chopped

1 leek, washed and thinly sliced

1 red pepper, seeded and chopped

225 g (8 oz) tomatoes, skinned and chopped

1.2 litres (2 pt) boiling water

50 g (2 oz) heart of cabbage, finely shredded

2.5 ml (½ tsp) thyme

1 bay leaf

salt and freshly ground black pepper

Soufflé Topping

20 g (¾ oz) butter

20 g (¾ oz) plain flour

150 ml (5 fl oz) milk

125 g (4 oz) Cheddar cheese, grated

2.5 ml (½ tsp) mustard powder

salt and freshly ground black pepper

3 eggs, separated

6 slices toast, cut into rounds the size of the soup dishes

 This is not as ambitious as it sounds! The soufflé topping floats on a round of toast on top of the soup and makes a very substantial starter for a winter's dinner party. The soup is very easy to prepare and benefits from being made in advance. The toast can also be prepared and cut into rounds, the eggs separated and the cheese grated. All that remains to be done, at the last minute, is to pour the soup into individual deep soup dishes (not plates), add the topping and wait for the compliments! Do try this one, as a rather special luncheon dish, followed by salads.

1. To make the soup, place the oil in a deep casserole and stir in the garlic, onion and sliced leek. Cover and microwave on HIGH for 5 minutes. Stir in the red pepper and tomatoes. Replace the cover and cook on HIGH for 5 minutes.

2. Pour over the boiling water, then add the cabbage, thyme, bay leaf and seasoning. Cover and cook in a preheated combination oven at 180°C with LOW power microwave for 40 minutes. Remove the bay leaf and pour the soup into the soup dishes. Set aside.

3. To prepare the soufflé, microwave the butter on HIGH for 30 seconds until melted. Stir in the flour, then gradually blend in the milk. Return to the microwave and cook on HIGH for 3 minutes, whisking thoroughly halfway through the cooking time, and again on completion.

4. Stir the cheese and mustard into the sauce, then beat in the egg yolks. Season to taste.

5. Whisk the egg whites until stiff, then fold into the sauce.

6. Float the rounds of toast on top of the soup and spoon the soufflé mixture on top. Cook in a preheated combination oven, using conventional heat only, at 200°C for 12–15 minutes or until risen and golden brown. Serve immediately.

FISH SOUP WITH PASTRY LID

SERVES 6

•

225 g (8 oz) shelled prawns

225 g (8 oz) plaice fillets, skinned
and roughly chopped

125 g (4 oz) cockles or mussels,
cooked and shelled

1 × 70 g (2¾ oz) can red
pimientos, drained and sliced

75 g (3 oz) button mushrooms,
sliced

600 ml (1 pt) fish stock

60 ml (4 tbsp) white wine

grated rind and juice of
½ lemon

15 ml (1 tbsp) chopped fresh
parsley

5 ml (1 tsp) fennel seeds, crushed

salt and freshly ground black
pepper

225 g (8 oz) puff pastry

egg or milk to glaze

 By using the combination oven, the soup and lid can be cooked simultaneously. The pastry acts as a lid to poach the fish. We used plaice, but whiting or grey mullet would be just as good. To prepare the dish for a dinner party, place all the ingredients except the stock in the soup dishes and have the pastry lids rolled out and ready. The soup can then be assembled and cooked at the last minute.

1. Divide the prawns, plaice, cockles or mussels, pimientos and mushrooms between 6 ovenproof soup dishes. (Use deep dishes if possible, not soup plates.)

2. Mix together the fish stock, wine, lemon rind and juice, parsley, fennel, salt and pepper. Pour over the fish in the dishes.

3. Roll out the pastry and cut a lid for each dish. Re-roll the trimmings and cut into long strips and fish shapes. Place a strip around the rim of each dish as an anchor for the lid. Make a small steam hole in the centre of each lid, brush with egg or milk and decorate with pastry fish shapes.

4. Bake in a preheated combination oven at 200°C with LOW power microwave for 15 minutes. Serve at once.

MALAYSIAN CHICKEN SOUP WITH RICE CUBES

SERVES 6
•

1 × 125 g (4 oz) packet boil-in-the-bag rice

600 ml (1 pt) boiling salted water

2 large chicken portions, skinned

1.2 litres (2 pt) cold water

1 small onion, roughly chopped

2.5 ml (½ tsp) turmeric

2.5 cm (1 in) piece of fresh ginger, peeled

2 cloves garlic, peeled

4 almonds

1 carrot, cooked

15 ml (1 tbsp) oil

salt

deep-fried onion rings (see Cook's tip) to serve

 Some Malaysian friends who were staying decided to cook for us and this is an adaptation of one of their dishes. The rice cubes can be made from any long-grain rice, simply over-cooked then pressed into a tin, weighted and left overnight. Other ingredients such as cooked, chopped peppers or spices can be added to the rice for extra interest. We use the boil-in-the-bag rice as it can then simply be weighted in the bag rather than in a tin. Both rice and soup should be made the previous day for the best results.

1. Place the rice in a deep casserole with the boiling, salted water. Cover and microwave on high for 20–25 minutes or until the rice is soft and beginning to lose its shape.

2. Drain the rice, and leaving it in the bag, squeeze out as much water as possible. Stand the bag on a plate, cover with a second plate and weight. Leave overnight.

3. To make the soup, place the chicken joints in a casserole with the water. Cover and cook in a preheated combination oven at 180°C with LOW power microwave for 30 minutes.

4. Remove the chicken joints, straining the stock into a clean casserole. Flake the chicken meat, then stir it back into the stock. Set aside.

5. Using a food processor or small chopper, grind together all the remaining ingredients, except the oil, salt and onion rings. Place the oil in a large bowl, stir in the chopped ingredients and microwave on HIGH for 2 minutes. Stir into the soup and season to taste with salt if necessary.

6. To serve, cut the rice into cubes and float in the soup. Reheat the soup and serve sprinkled with deep fried onion rings.

—— COOK'S TIP——

Deep fried onion is a useful addition to many Indian dishes. Cut several large onions into rings, separate them out, and deep-fry in hot oil until caramel-coloured. Drain and sprinkle with salt. When quite cold, store in an airtight jar and use as a garnish for rice, dhal and curries.

PARSNIP AND ORANGE SOUP

SERVES 6

•

30 ml (2 tbsp) sunflower oil

1 small onion, chopped

1 small potato, peeled and diced

450 g (1 lb) parsnips, peeled and diced

600 ml (1 pt) chicken stock (a good-quality stock cube may be used)

150 ml (5 fl oz) orange juice

½ orange

salt and freshly ground black pepper

150 ml (5 fl oz) single cream

julienne strips of orange peel to garnish (optional)

 This is a delicious and very cheap soup to make. The texture is very smooth and the flavour not at all parsnipy! It is quite grand enough to serve as a dinner party starter or it will serve 4 with crusty brown bread for lunch.

1. Mix the oil, onion, potato and parsnips together in a large bowl. Cover and microwave on HIGH for 8 minutes stirring once or twice. Add the boiling stock and orange juice. Remove the peel from the ½ orange in a long strip, using a potato peeler. Add the peel to the bowl and microwave on HIGH for 15 minutes, stirring once or twice.

2. Purée the soup in a blender or food processor, then, using a soup ladle, press through a sieve, into a clear bowl.

3. Season the soup and add the cream. Stir in a little extra hot stock if it is too thick. Reheat but do not boil before serving.

4. If you wish to use orange julienne as a garnish, soften the strips in a little boiling water for 5 minutes, pat dry on paper towels and float them on the top of the soup.

WATERCRESS SOUP

SERVES 6
•
1 × 125 g (4 oz) onion, finely chopped

50 g (2 oz) butter

125 g (4 oz) peeled potatoes

2 bunches of watercress

1 litre (1¾ pt) hot chicken or vegetable stock

salt and freshly ground black pepper

60 ml (4 tbsp) double cream

Watercress soup, with its attractive pale green colour is always popular. It is ideal for entertaining because it can be made in advance and reheated. To really make it memorable we serve it with Stilton tart (see page 117) which seems to be especially popular with male guests.

1. Place the onion in a large bowl with the butter. Microwave on HIGH for 4 minutes. Grate the potatoes and add to the onion mixture. Microwave on HIGH for 4 minutes.

2. Wash the cress and chop roughly, reserving a few leaves for garnish. Add to the onion mixture, stir well and microwave on HIGH for 5 minutes, stirring once.

3. Add the stock and cook on HIGH power for 10 minutes, stirring once.

4. Pureé the soup in a blender or food processor, then push it through a sieve into a clean bowl. Reheat if necessary for the best result.

5. Season to taste and stir in the cream. Float a reserved watercress leaf on top of each bowl of soup – and serve immediately.

FENNEL AND ANISEED BREAD ROLLS

MAKES 16 ROLLS
•
450 g (1 lb) strong brown flour

225 g (8 oz) strong white flour

5 ml (1 tsp) salt

25 g (1 oz) margarine

7.5 ml (1½ tsp) fennel seeds

7.5 ml (1½ tsp) aniseed

1 sachet easy-blend dried yeast

450 ml (¾ pt) hand-hot water

Having once tasted fennel and aniseed bread in a Swedish restaurant, we determined to devise a recipe, and the following is our interpretation. The bread has a wonderful flavour and complements soups or starters, especially those with a fish base. Your guests will be intrigued to know what the flavour is!

1. Mix the flours and salt in a large bowl and rub in the fat.

2. Crush the fennel seeds and aniseed with a mortar and pestle or grind quickly in a coffee grinder. Stir into the flour with the dried yeast.

3. Add the water, stir to a dough, then turn on to a floured board and knead for 5 minutes until smooth and elastic. Put the dough into an oiled plastic bag and leave to rise in a warm place until doubled in bulk.

4. Turn the dough out, knead again for 2 minutes then divide into 16 portions.

Shape each into a roll. Arrange the rolls in a 4 × 4 square on a greased baking dish, allowing each roll to just touch its neighbour.

5. Prove the dough again in a warm place until well risen, then bake in a pre-heated combination oven at 220°C, with LOW power microwave for 15 minutes.

—— COOK'S TIP——

The rolls freeze very successfully, so can be made well in advance of a dinner party. Remove from the freezer 30 minutes before serving and pop them into a hot oven to warm through just before your guests are seated.

STUFFED MUSHROOMS

SERVES 4
•
16 large button mushrooms, wiped

50 g (2 oz) butter

1 small onion, finely chopped

125 g (4 oz) bacon, chopped

125 g (4 oz) tomatoes, chopped

25 g (1 oz) brown breadcrumbs

15 ml (1 tbsp) chopped fresh parsley

salt and freshly ground black pepper

This recipe was originally developed as a breakfast idea, using the large flat mushrooms. It can also be used as a light luncheon or supper dish, but here we use button mushrooms in individual dishes as a starter. Prepare the mushrooms to step 3 in advance, then cook and serve at the last minute. Anchovies can be used instead of bacon.

1. Remove and chop the mushroom stalks, then place 4 mushrooms, cups uppermost on each of 4 individual plates.

2. Microwave the butter in a dish on HIGH for 1½ minutes or until melted. Stir in the chopped mushroom stalks, onion and bacon, cover and cook on HIGH for 3 minutes. Add the remaining ingredients and mix thoroughly.

3. Spoon the mixture on top of each mushroom. Microwave, 2 plates at a time for 3 minutes on HIGH. Serve at once.

ASPARAGUS WITH HOLLANDAISE SAUCE

SERVES 4
•
450 g (1 lb) fresh asparagus

60 ml (4 tbsp) water

125 g (4 oz) butter

2 egg yolks

30 ml (2 tbsp) white wine vinegar

salt and freshly ground black pepper

Even though we live in an asparagus growing area, with friends who own an asparagus farm, we never tire of the wonderful flavour of this vegetable and only wish it were readily available for a longer period each year. This is a traditional recipe made even more tempting with a hollandaise sauce prepared in the microwave. It is a must to serve during the asparagus season. Frozen asparagus, (but not canned) is an acceptable substitute. Keep a very careful eye on the sauce, checking regularly, as it will curdle if the heat is too sudden or too high. If this happens, the sauce can sometimes be saved by beating in an ice cube or a tablespoon of cold water.

1. Trim the asparagus spears and lay them in a single layer in a shallow dish. Pour over the water, cover and microwave on HIGH for 6–8 minutes or until tender. Leave to stand, covered.

2. Microwave the butter in a bowl on MEDIUM for 2 minutes or until melted, then whisk in the egg yolks, vinegar and seasoning.

3. Return the bowl to the microwave and cook on MEDIUM for 1½ minutes, whisking after 30 seconds and again every 15 seconds until thickened.

4. Drain the asparagus and serve with the hollandaise sauce.

SPICED CITRUS SUNFLOWER

SERVES 4
2 pink grapefruit

2 large Jaffa oranges

2 sweeties

2.5 ml (½ tsp) cinnamon

20 ml (4 tsp) demerara sugar

45 ml (3 tbsp) cream sherry

When planning a dinner party, it is very easy to be over-enthusiastic with cream, butter and wine, resulting in a very rich meal. It is good, therefore, to have a simple, refreshing starter in your repertoire to complement a rich main course. This is a very simple but attractive idea using citrus fruits of different colours. The sweetie is a type of grapefruit, which lives up to its name! It looks like an ordinary grapefruit but is less bitter. If sweeties are not available, substitute grapefruit.

1. Peel the pink grapefruit, oranges and sweeties with a sharp knife, taking care to remove all the pith. Cut them carefully into segments.

2. Arrange the citrus segments in alternate colours on individual serving plates.

3. Heat two at a time in the microwave on HIGH for 2 minutes.

4. Mix the cinnamon and sugar together and sprinkle over the fruit, then do the same with the sherry.

CHICKEN AND MUSHROOM MOULD

SERVES 6–8

•

225 g (8 oz) fresh leaf spinach or 1 lettuce, separated into leaves

cucumber slices, to garnish

Filling

25 g (1 oz) butter

1 onion, finely chopped

125 g (4 oz) button mushrooms, wiped and sliced

10 ml (2 tsp) dried oregano

salt and freshly ground black pepper

225 g (8 oz) cooked chicken, chopped

3 tomatoes, seeded and chopped

¼ cucumber, finely chopped

175 g (6 oz) Edam cheese, finely grated

60 ml (4 tbsp) mayonnaise

 This unusual dish makes a very good starter or light luncheon dish with salad. It also looks very attractive on the buffet table. Vary the recipe by using seafood for the filling instead of chicken, adding tomato purée and a dash of Tabasco. Make the mould in the morning to serve the same evening.

1. If using spinach leaves, blanch them in boiling water and drain thoroughly. Line a 23 cm (9 in) sandwich cake tin with the spinach or lettuce leaves, leaving enough hanging over the edge to cover the filling.

2. Microwave the butter in a large bowl on HIGH for 1 minute or until melted. Add the onion, mushrooms and oregano, with salt and pepper to taste. Microwave on HIGH for 4 minutes, stirring halfway through the cooking time. Leave to cool.

3. When cold add all the remaining ingredients and mix well. Spoon the mixture into the prepared tin. Cover with the overlapping leaves and leave to set in the refrigerator.

4. Unmould the dish on to a serving plate, garnish with cucumber slices then cut into wedges to serve.

VEGETABLE TERRINE WITH PIMIENTO PURÉE

SERVES 6–8
•

1 × 225 g (8 oz) aubergine

15 ml (1 tbsp) finely chopped onion

1 clove garlic, crushed

15 ml (1 tbsp) chopped fresh parsley

15 ml (1 tbsp) single cream

3 eggs

salt and freshly ground black pepper

225 g (8 oz) carrots, peeled and sliced

175 g (6 oz) tomatoes, skinned and chopped

2.5 ml (½ tsp) cayenne

125 g (4 oz) green pepper, seeded and chopped

225 g (8 oz) courgettes, sliced

7.5 ml (½ tbsp) water

2.5 ml (½ tsp) tarragon

Pimiento Purée

1 × 370 g (13 oz) can pimientos

10 ml (2 tsp) sugar

salt and freshly ground black pepper

The combination of colours and flavours in this terrine makes it an unusual and attractive starter or light luncheon dish. It should be made the day before, then thoroughly chilled and served with a nutty granary bread.

1. Score the aubergine around the middle with a sharp knife, then microwave on HIGH for 5 minutes. Cut the aubergine in half and scoop out all the flesh into a blender or food processor. Add the onion, garlic, parsley, cream, 1 egg and seasoning. Blend until smooth.

2. Pour the mixture into a greased 900 g (2 lb) loaf dish, then set aside.

3. Place the carrots and tomatoes in a dish, cover and microwave on HIGH for 8 minutes, or until tender, stirring occasionally. Tip into a blender or food processor, add the cayenne, 1 egg and seasoning to taste, then blend until smooth. Pour carefully over the aubergine mixture, then set aside.

4. Place the chopped pepper and courgette slices in a dish with the water. Cover and microwave on HIGH for 7 minutes, stirring occasionally. Pour into a blender or food processor, add the tarragon, the final egg and seasoning to taste, then blend until smooth. Pour carefully over the back of a spoon on to the carrot mixture.

5. Cover with buttered greaseproof paper and cook in a preheated combination oven at 175°C with LOW power microwave for 15 minutes or until a skewer inserted in the middle comes out clean. Leave to cool in the dish, then chill in the refrigerator.

6. To make the purée, place the pimiento with the can juices in a blender or food processor and blend until smooth. Season to taste, with the sugar, salt and pepper.

7. To serve, invert the terrine on to a platter and slice to show the vegetable layers. Serve with the pimiento purée.

FISH TERRINE WITH TOMATO COULIS

SERVES 8
•
125 g (4 oz) fillets of plaice or sole

15 ml (1 tbsp) milk

225 g (8 oz) frozen spinach, defrosted and thoroughly drained

1 × 200 g (7 oz) can pink salmon, drained, bones removed and flaked

15 g (½ oz) gelatine

45 ml (3 tbsp) lemon juice

150 ml (5 fl oz) double cream

salt and freshly ground black pepper

15 ml (1 tbsp) tomato purée

2 egg whites

Tomato coulis

1 × 397 g (14 oz) can chopped tomatoes, blended or sieved

5 ml (1 tsp) dried dill

30 ml (2 tbsp) wine vinegar

salt and freshly ground black pepper

 Layered terrines always look impressive, but they also look complicated to make. This is a very simple one which is also economical. An all–fish terrine can be made, using smoked fish instead of spinach. This also looks very attractive, although there is a danger that the smoked fish flavour may dominate. To serve for a dinner party, prepare the terrine in the morning, unmould during the afternoon and keep chilled in the refrigerator.

1. Place the white fish in a dish with the milk, cover and microwave on HIGH for 2 minutes. Drain, and flake.

2. Place the white fish, spinach, and salmon in 3 separate bowls.

3. Sprinkle the gelatine over the lemon juice, stand for 2 minutes, then microwave on HIGH for 30 seconds or until dissolved. Divide the gelatine mixture between the 3 bowls and mix each thoroughly.

4. Whip the cream until stiff and divide between the 3 bowls, mixing thoroughly. Season to taste. Stir the tomato purée into the salmon mixture, to give a good pink colour. Whisk the egg whites until stiff, then divide between the bowls and fold into each mixture carefully.

5. Grease a 450 g (1 lb) loaf tin thoroughly. Spoon the white fish mixture into the base of the tin and smooth over with a palette knife. Gently spoon the spinach mixture over the white fish and again smooth over. Repeat with the salmon mixture. Chill the terrine in the refrigerator until set.

6. To make the tomato coulis, place all the ingredients in a bowl and microwave on HIGH for 8 minutes, then pour into a sauce boat and chill.

7. Dip the loaf tin in hot water, then invert the terrine on to a serving dish. Chill until required. To serve, cut into slices and serve with the tomato coulis.

PORK AND ORANGE TERRINE

SERVES 8 AS A STARTER
•
225 g (8 oz) streaky bacon rashers

1 medium onion, finely chopped

1 clove garlic, crushed

25 g (1 oz) butter

30 ml (2 tbsp) dry sherry

450 g (1 lb) minced pork

175 g (6 oz) lamb's liver, finely diced

grated rind of 1 orange

5 ml (1 tsp) oregano

salt and freshly ground black pepper

1 egg

 A meat terrine like this can be surprisingly economical to make. It is useful as a supper or lunch dish or, if served with a little lettuce, radicchio and orange segments, a beautiful starter. Make this a few days in advance if you like. It will store well in the refrigerator. Do not freeze because it tends to become watery when defrosted.

1. Stretch the bacon rashers with the back of a knife and use to line a 675 g (1½ lb) loaf dish.

2. Put the onion, garlic and butter into a bowl and microwave on HIGH for 4 minutes. Stir in the sherry and microwave on HIGH for 1 minute. Set aside to cool.

3. Stir in the remaining ingredients and mix well. Microwave a small ball of the mixture on HIGH for ½–1 minute, taste and adjust seasoning, if necessary.

4. Pack the mixture into the bacon lined dish. Cover with greaseproof paper and cook in a preheated combination oven at 160°C with LOW power microwave for 30 minutes.

5. Place a 1.8 kg (4 lb) weight on top and cool. Chill overnight in the refrigerator before serving.

TURKEY AND VEGETABLE LAYERED TERRINE

SERVES 6–8 AS A STARTER OR 4
AS A MAIN COURSE
•
125 g (4 oz) carrots, peeled and cut
into fine julienne strips
(matchsticks)

15 ml (1 tbsp) water

50 g (2 oz) broccoli florets

1 small courgette, finely sliced

175 g (6 oz) ham

350 g (12 oz) turkey breast

1 egg, beaten

150 ml (5 fl oz) single cream

salt and freshly ground black
pepper

This terrine could be cooked entirely on HIGH but we found that this tends to make it a little tough. It looks very pretty and is surprisingly easy to make. If you wish to serve the terrine cold make it the day before you need it, loosen the sides before chilling it, and then stand the terrine in hot water before serving so that it turns out easily. Slice with a sharp knife before serving.

1. Put the carrots into a dish with the water. Cover and microwave on HIGH for 3 minutes. Add the broccoli and cook on HIGH for 2 minutes, then add the courgette slices (without stirring) and cook on HIGH for a further 3 minutes. Drain without mixing.

2. Mince the ham and turkey together or chop very finely by hand or in a food processor. Add the beaten egg, cream and seasoning to taste. Mix well.

3. Lightly grease a 600 ml (1 pt) or slightly larger loaf dish and arrange two thirds of the carrots and courgettes in a pattern on the base.

4. Cover with half the meat mixture, arrange the remaining vegetables on top, then cover with the remaining meat mixture, pressing down well.

5. Cover and microwave on HIGH for 5 minutes. Reduce the power to MEDIUM and cook for 12 minutes more. Leave to cool for 10 minutes before turning out. Serve hot or cold, cut into slices so that the layers can be admired.

SOLE AND BACON ROLLS

SERVES 4
•
1 large or 2 small sole(s)

12 very thinly sliced unsmoked bacon rashers, rind removed

freshly ground black pepper

15 ml (1 tbsp) lemon juice

25 g (1 oz) Cheddar cheese, grated

This unusual combination of surf and turf is certain to be popular. It may seem a bit fiddly but the rolls may be made a couple of hours in advance and kept covered in the refrigerator until required. Just before serving, season, sprinkle with lemon juice and cheese and cook.

1. Fillet the fish and cut into strips 5 × 7.5 cm (2 × 3 in); you should have about 24 pieces.

2. Stretch the bacon rashers with the back of a knife and cut each rasher in half. They should be approximately the same length as the fish.

3. Lay a piece of fish on each piece of bacon. Season with pepper and roll up. Arrange in a shallow dish with the ends underneath and sprinkle with the lemon juice and cheese.

4. Cover and microwave on HIGH for 4 minutes or until the fish is flaky. If extra time is needed rearrange the fish rolls.

5. Serve on individual serving plates with the juices poured over. Garnish with parsley, if liked.

PRAWN MOUSSELINES

SERVES 6
•
50 g (2 oz) smoked salmon

450 g (1 lb) frozen prawns, defrosted

3 egg whites

200 ml (7 fl oz) double cream

salt and freshly ground black pepper

150 ml (5 fl oz) single cream

a squeeze of lemon juice

5 ml (1 tsp) tomato purée

To Garnish

6 whole prawns

sprigs of fresh herbs

This is a delicate pastel-coloured prawn mousse, with a creamy smoked salmon sauce. A mousseline should traditionally be cooked in a bain marie but this is not necessary with the combination oven. Mousselines are usually served hot, but this recipe works well hot or cold. If served hot, the sauce should only be warmed; do not boil or it may separate. If served cold, prepare in advance and chill in the refrigerator for several hours.

1. Cut half the smoked salmon into narrow strips. Place 2 strips in the base of each of 6 buttered ramekins. Reserve the remaining salmon for the sauce.

2. Drain the prawns thoroughly on paper towels, then mince (a food processor is ideal for this). Transfer the minced prawns to a bowl.

3. Break up the egg whites with a fork, then beat into the prawns. Beat in the cream and season to taste.

4. Pour into the prepared ramekins and bake in a preheated combination oven at 180°C with LOW power microwave for 15 minutes. Allow to cool for a few minutes before turning out.

5. To make the sauce, place the remaining smoked salmon in a blender or food processor. Add the cream, lemon juice and tomato purée and process until smooth. Add seasoning to taste. Warm through if the mousselines are to be served hot.

6. Serve the mousselines on individual plates surrounded by sauce. Garnish each with a whole prawn and fresh herbs.

CHICKEN LIVER MOUSSE WITH GREEN PEPPERCORNS, SULTANAS AND THYME

SERVES 8
•
350 g (12 oz) chicken livers covered with milk and left for 2 hours

225 g (8 oz) unsmoked streaky bacon rashers, rinds removed

30 ml (2 tbsp) dry sherry

30 ml (2 tbsp) port

25 g (1 oz) sultanas

2.5 ml (½ tsp) dried thyme

125 g (4 oz) butter, melted

2 egg yolks

30 ml (2 tbsp) green peppercorns

fresh thyme and peppercorns to garnish

Melba toast to serve (see Cook's tip)

 This mousse is very rich but very light in texture. Normally this does not need any seasoning, because the bacon and peppercorns add all that is necessary. A word of warning however: green peppercorns vary in strength, so if you buy a jar taste one first. If it seems very hot by all means reduce the quantity. Make the terrine the day before it is needed and do not freeze it because it goes watery. The Melba toast can be made up to a week in advance, if you store it in an airtight tin or bag.

1. Place the chicken livers in a shallow dish. Add milk to cover and set aside for 2 hours.

2. Stretch the bacon rashers with the back of a knife and use to line a 1 litre (1¾ pt) terrine or loaf dish.

3. Put the sherry, port and sultanas in a bowl and microwave on HIGH for 2 minutes. Set aside.

4. Drain the chicken livers, discarding the milk, and place in a blender or food processor. Add the thyme and blend until smooth, gradually adding the melted butter and egg yolks.

5. Drain the sultanas, adding the liquid to the liver mixture. Mix the sultanas with the peppercorns. Pour a little of the liver mixture into the terrine, sprinkle on some of the peppercorns and sultanas and repeat until all the mixture is used up.

6. Cover with greaseproof paper and bake in a preheated combination oven at

170°C with LOW power microwave for 35 minutes. Leave the mousse to cool, then chill overnight in the refrigerator.

7. Slice, using a knife that has been dipped in boiling water, and garnish with a sprig of thyme and a few peppercorns. Serve with Melba toast.

—— COOK'S TIP——

Melba toast is very easy to make: simply toast medium to thick sliced bread on each side, then cut the crusts off. With a sharp knife slice the bread through the middle, exposing two un-toasted sides. As you toast these the toast will curl up. Because it is so delicious allow two slices of bread (four pieces of Melba toast) per person.

SMOKED SALMON MOUSSE

SERVES 6
•
125 g (4 oz) smoked salmon

30 ml (2 tbsp) lemon juice

30 ml (2 tbsp) milk

freshly ground black pepper

5 ml (1 tsp) tomato purée (optional)

5 ml (1 tsp) gelatine

15 ml (1 tbsp) water

150 ml (5 fl oz) double cream

*brown Melba toast
(see previous recipe) to serve*

To Garnish

6 small smoked salmon strips

fresh parsley

lemon wedges

 The microwave is hardly necessary for this mousse, but it is so delicious and so good for entertaining that we felt it could not be missed out. It also gave us the excuse to test it a few more times! This makes a very soft mousse; if you wish to turn it out, increase the gelatine to 15 ml (1 tbsp). It only takes a couple of hours to set, so make it no longer than the day before you want to serve it.

1. Combine the salmon, lemon juice, milk and pepper in a blender or food processor and purée until smooth. You will have to keep pushing the mixture on to the blades with a spatula.

2. If the colour at this stage is not pink enough add the tomato purée; this will depend on the type of salmon you have used.

3. Sprinkle the gelatine over the water, stand for 2 minutes, then microwave on HIGH power for 30 seconds or until dissolved.

4. Whip the cream to soft peaks. Fold the puréed salmon, cream and gelatine mixture together, pour into a bowl and leave to set in the refrigerator.

5. Serve spoonsful of mousse on a large plate garnished with smoked salmon strips, lemon wedges and parsley. Brown Melba toast makes a good accompaniment.

OPPOSITE
Asparagus with hollandaise sauce (page 24); Marinated mint and orange lamb (page 52); Apple in the clouds (page 94).

OVERLEAF
Watercress soup (page 22); Stilton tart (page 117); Oranges with caramel cream (page 109).

SMOKED HADDOCK AND MUSHROOM CRACKERS

SERVES 4

•

4 small fillets of smoked haddock

4 sheets of filo pastry

75 g (3 oz) butter, melted (see Cook's tip)

125 g (4 oz) button mushrooms, wiped and sliced

125 g (4 oz) Gouda cheese, cut into 4 slices

freshly ground black pepper

 This is a very easy starter or supper dish. It looks very pretty and avoids any anxiety over portion control. All the ingredients can be prepared in advance, but the crackers should be rolled up no more than half an hour before cooking. Filo pastry dries out very quickly. Keep unused sheets covered with a damp tea towel while you work.

1. Skin the fish and cut each fillet in half widthways.

2. Brush a sheet of filo pastry with butter. Fold in half widthways and brush with butter again. In the middle of the filo rectangle, about 5 cm (2 in) in from the folded edge lay a piece of fish. Pile on a quarter of the mushrooms, top with a slice of cheese, season with pepper and top with another piece of fish.

3. Quickly roll up the filo and pinch the ends together to make a cracker shape. Brush well with butter and put on a buttered baking sheet suitable for your oven while making three more crackers in the same way.

4. Bake in a preheated combination oven at 200°C with LOW power microwave for 12 minutes or until crisp. Serve immediately.

—— COOK'S TIP ——

Melt the butter in the microwave on HIGH for 1 minute.

PREVIOUS PAGE
Stuffed mushrooms (page 23); Casserole of duck in cider (page 62) with Savoury brown rice (page 81); Chocolate walnut pie (page 91).

OPPOSITE
Vegetable terrine with pimiento purée (page 26); Chicken with Roquefort in filo pastry (page 61); Celery au gratin (page 74); Grape and almond tart (page 97).

MAIN COURSES

FISH

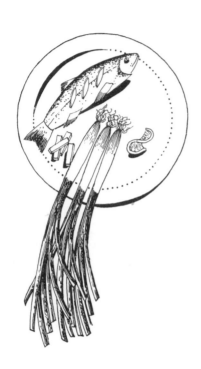

*T*HE RECIPES IN this section have been planned as a main course, but by cutting the quantities or dividing into smaller portions, many can serve as starters. You will find more delicious fish recipes in the chapter on Soups, starters and snacks.

With the growing interest in health, fish, with its low fat content, is becoming a popular source of protein. This rising popularity means that fresh fish is becoming more readily available in the high street and in the supermarket. When buying fresh fish, check that the flesh is firm, the eyes are shiny and that it does not have a strong smell. Fresh fish is infinitely preferable to frozen. If it is not available, however, most of our recipes allow for the substitution of frozen fish. Remember though to defrost and drain thoroughly before use or the resulting dish may lack flavour and be swamped.

We include an easy fish stock recipe to use up fish trimmings. This can be stored in convenient quantities in the freezer and will enhance the flavour of fish dishes.

FISH STOCK

MAKES 900 ml (1½ pt)
•
450 g (1 lb) fish pieces,

1 onion, chopped

30 ml (2 tbsp) sunflower oil

1 carrot, sliced

1 stick celery, sliced

2 bay leaves

4 parsley stalks

1 litre (1¾ pt) boiling water

salt and freshly ground pepper

In many fish dishes you will find the instruction to "use fish stock". Often this is unavailable and the thought of boiling up large quantities of fish to make a stock can be daunting, not to mention smelly! This is a quick and easy method for making the stock in the combination oven, using the microwave. Any unused stock can be frozen. In an emergency, chicken stock makes an acceptable substitute.

1. Chop up the fish pieces and put them into a large bowl with the onion and oil. Stir, then microwave on HIGH for 5 minutes.

2. Add the carrot and celery slices, the bay leaves, parsley stalks and boiling water, and microwave on HIGH for 15 minutes, stirring once or twice.

3. Strain the stock, return to the clean bowl and microwave on HIGH for 10

minutes. Season as necessary. If a stronger stock is required reduce by micro-waving on HIGH until of the desired strength.

4.   Use as directed in fish recipes needing stock.

CRAB SOUFFLÉ LAYER

SERVES 4
•
25 g (1 oz) butter

25 g (1 oz) plain flour

300 ml (½ pt) milk

*salt and freshly ground black
pepper*

1.25 ml (¼ tsp) cayenne

125 g (4 oz) dark crab meat, flaked

3 egg yolks

2 egg whites

125 g (4 oz) white crab meat

25 g (1 oz) Cheddar cheese, grated

*25 g (1 oz) fresh brown
breadcrumbs*

This is a light, almost mousse-like soufflé which does not rise much, but sets to a delicious, light texture. We use frozen crab meat which comes in a 450 g (1 lb) pack, half white and half dark meat. It is much better than canned crab and can be cut while frozen, so that all the meat does not need to be used at once. The soufflé may be prepared in advance to the end of step 2. Just before serving, whisk the egg whites, fold them in with the remaining ingredients and combination cook.

1.   Place the butter in a bowl and microwave on HIGH for 1 minute or until melted. Stir in the flour, then gradually blend in the milk. Cook on HIGH for 4 minutes, whisking halfway through the cooking time and again on completion.

2.   Season the sauce and add the cayenne. Beat in the dark crab meat and egg yolks.

3.   Whisk the egg whites until stiff, then fold into the sauce mixture. Pour half the mixture into a buttered 18 cm (7 in) soufflé dish.

4.   Break up the white crab meat with a fork and sprinkle over the soufflé. Top with the remaining soufflé mixture.

5.   Mix the cheese and breadcrumbs and sprinkle over the top of the soufflé layer. Bake in a preheated combination oven at 180°C with LOW power microwave for 20 minutes.

TURBANE OF WHITING

SERVES 4–8

•

25 g (1 oz) butter, plus extra to grease mould and paper

8 whiting or plaice fillets, skinned

1 small onion, finely chopped

75 g (3 oz) button mushrooms, wiped and chopped

75 g (3 oz) fresh white breadcrumbs

grated rind of 1 lemon

15 ml (1 tbsp) chopped fresh parsley

2 eggs, lightly beaten

300 ml (½ pt) milk

salt and freshly ground black pepper

Sauce

150 ml (5 fl oz) mayonnaise

150 ml (5 fl oz) natural yogurt

15 ml (1 tbsp) tomato purée

dash of Tabasco

pinch of tarragon

50 g (2 oz) peeled prawns

To garnish

watercress

4 whole prawns

lemon slices

This is so simple to do, but will always impress your guests! It always turns out of the ring without any trouble, so forget about failures. The turbane makes a substantial main course for 4, a fish course for 6 or a starter for 8. Go to town on the garnish as it really does set the dish off to perfection. The turbane can be cooked in advance and reheated in the mould. Mix the sauce ingredients and heat at the last minute.

1. Butter a 1.2 litre (2 pt) glass or heatproof plastic ring mould, then line with the fish fillets, skinned side up. Do not worry if the fillets overlap the mould: they will be folded in later.

2. Microwave 25 g (1 oz) butter in a bowl on HIGH for 1 minute or until melted. Stir in the onion and microwave on HIGH for 2 minutes.

3. Stir in the mushrooms and microwave on HIGH for 2 minutes more. Add the breadcrumbs, lemon rind, parsley, eggs and milk and mix well. Season, then spoon into the fish-lined mould.

4. Fold the overlapping ends of fish fillet in and cover with buttered grease-proof paper, butter-side down.

5. Bake in a preheated combination oven at 180°C with LOW power microwave for 20 minutes. Leave to stand while making the sauce.

6. Combine all the sauce ingredients in a small bowl. Microwave on HIGH for 2–3 minutes or until heated through. Unmould the fish on to a serving dish, coat with sauce and serve garnished with watercress, whole prawns and lemon slices.

PLAICE WITH PRAWNS AND MUSHROOMS

SERVES 4
•

8 plaice fillets, skinned

butter to grease dish

125 g (4 oz) mushrooms, wiped and sliced

125 g (4 oz) peeled prawns

15 ml (1 tbsp) chopped fresh parsley

salt and freshly ground black pepper

30 ml (2 tbsp) white wine

150 ml (5 fl oz) double cream

lemon slices and fresh parsley to garnish

This gourmet-style recipe can be prepared in minutes, thanks to the speed of the microwave. Serve it in individual portions as a starter or even as a fish course for an extra-special meal. Prepare the dish in advance, pouring over the wine, but not the cream. Cover and leave in the refrigerator until the last minute, then pour over the cream and cook.

1. Arrange the plaice fillets in a shallow, buttered dish.

2. Sprinkle over the mushrooms, prawns and parsley.

3. Season to taste then pour over the wine and cream. Cover and microwave on HIGH for 8–10 minutes, depending on the size of the fish. Garnish and serve at once.

FILLETS OF PLAICE WITH SMOKED SALMON

SERVES 6
•
6 × 175 g (6 oz) whole fillets of plaice

75 g (3 oz) sliced smoked salmon

salt and freshly ground black pepper

60 ml (4 tbsp) dry white wine

150 ml (5 fl oz) fish stock (see page 39)

15 g (½ oz) butter

15 g (½ oz) plain flour

60 ml (4 tbsp) double cream

chopped fresh parsley to garnish

This is a very delicate fish main course which also makes a very good starter if smaller fillets are used. If plaice is unobtainable use sole instead. Prepare the dish in advance by rolling up the fish, adding the wine and setting it aside until ready to cook. Make the sauce with additional wine but do not add the cream. Cover (see Cook's tip). When ready to serve, cook the fish, discarding the cooking liquid. Reheat the sauce, add the cream and serve.

1. Skin the plaice fillets. Spread them flat on a clean work surface, skinned side uppermost. Sprinkle with the black pepper and cover with the smoked salmon, reserving a few strips for garnish.

2. Roll up the fillets and secure each with a wooden toothpick. Arrange the rolls in a shallow dish and pour over the wine. Cover and microwave on HIGH for 5 minutes, rearranging the rolls halfway. Test the fish. If not cooked, microwave for 1 minute more on HIGH.

3. Drain the wine into a bowl, add the stock and microwave on HIGH for 2 minutes. Cream the butter and flour together and whisk into the hot stock mixture. Microwave on HIGH for 2 minutes until thickened and boiling.

4. Season to taste and stir in the cream. To serve, cut the fish rolls in half lengthways and pour the sauce around. Garnish with the reserved salmon and a little chopped parsley.

—— COOK'S TIP——

To prevent the formation of a skin on the sauce, cover the surface with damp greaseproof paper or cling film.

POACHED SALMON WITH SAUCE RAVIGOTE

SERVES 4
•
4 salmon fillets

bouquet garni (fresh parsley stalks, tarragon, fennel and chives, tied together)

2 shallots, finely chopped

75 ml (5 tbsp) white wine

15 ml (1 tbsp) lemon juice

salt and freshly ground black pepper

fresh herbs to garnish

Sauce

70 g (2¾ oz) butter

15 ml (1 tbsp) plain flour

2 egg yolks

300 ml (½ pt) hot water

5 ml (1 tsp) green mustard

5 ml (1 tsp) chopped chives

5 ml (1 tsp) chopped tarragon

5 ml (1 tsp) chopped fennel

salt and freshly ground black pepper

Lightly poached salmon steaks in a fresh herb sauce – a delightful combination. Ideally fresh herbs should be used for the best results. The sauce, which is a mock hollandaise, is the most tricky part of the recipe, but this can be prepared in advance, apart for the addition of the reduced cooking liquor from the salmon. Serve the poached salmon, with the sauce, as soon as possible after cooking. New potatoes and cooked cucumber or courgette are ideal accompaniments.

1. First make the sauce. Microwave 20 g (¾ oz) of the butter in a large jug or bowl on HIGH for 30 seconds or until melted. Stir in the flour and cook for 30 seconds more to make a roux.

2. Whisk the egg yolks lightly. Gradually add the water, whisking constantly. Add the eggs and water to the roux, whisk, then microwave on HIGH for 1 minute. Whisk again, then microwave on HIGH for 1 minute more. Whisk again and microwave on HIGH for 15–30 seconds or until starting to thicken.

3. Remove from the oven and whisk in the remaining butter, a little at a time. Whisk in the remaining sauce ingredients with the seasoning. Set the sauce aside.

4. To cook the salmon, place it in a shallow dish with the fresh herbs and shallots. Pour over the wine and lemon juice and season to taste. Cover, and cook in a preheated combination oven at 180°C with LOW power microwave for 15–18 minutes. Turn once during the cooking time. Remove the salmon and keep warm.

5. Reduce the cooking liquor by microwaving on HIGH for about 2 minutes or until only 15 ml (1 tbsp) remains. Strain into the sauce, stirring until smooth.

6. Reheat the sauce, if necessary, being careful not to let it boil, then pour over the salmon, garnish with fresh herbs, and serve.

STUFFED RED FISH WITH SPINACH SAUCE

SERVES 4

•

125 g (4 oz) butter

1 small onion, chopped

1 leek, washed and sliced

150 ml (5 fl oz) fish stock
(see page 39)

45 ml (3 tbsp) dry vermouth

125 g (4 oz) frozen leaf spinach,
defrosted

salt and freshly ground black
pepper

1 × 1.5 kg (3 lb) red fish, scaled and
gutted but left whole

45 ml (3 tbsp) double cream

Stuffing

50 g (2 oz) lean bacon rashers,
chopped

1 small onion, chopped

25 g (1 oz) butter

125 g (4 oz) button mushrooms,
wiped and chopped

50 g (2 oz) fresh breadcrumbs

125 g (4 oz) frozen leaf spinach,
defrosted

1 egg, beaten

salt and freshly ground black
pepper

 Red fish is becoming more widely available. It is also much less expensive than many other varieties of fish. Our fishmonger recommends that it be cleaned just prior to cooking and always cooked with the head on. This may mean that you will have to curl it to fit it into your oven. You may wish to use the sauce with other fish dishes, as it is so delicious. The stuffing may be made in advance, as may the sauce, but the fish should be stuffed and cooked just before serving.

1. Put 50 g (2 oz) of the butter into a casserole with the onion and leek and microwave on HIGH for 4 minutes, stirring once. Add the fish stock and cook for 6 minutes on HIGH, then stir in the vermouth.

2. Squeeze the spinach to remove as much liquid as possible. Add it to the stock mixture and mix well. Purée in a blender or food processor until smooth, season to taste and set aside.

3. Make the stuffing: combine the bacon and onion in a dish. Add the butter and microwave on HIGH for 3 minutes. Stir in the chopped mushrooms and microwave for 2 minutes more, then add the breadcrumbs. Drain the spinach thoroughly, chop it roughly, then stir it into the stuffing with the beaten egg. Season to taste.

4. Wash the fish and dry thoroughly with paper towels. Stuff the cavity, taking care not to overfill, Make the remaining stuffing into balls the size of walnuts.

5. Microwave the remaining 50 g (2 oz) butter on HIGH for 1 minute in a dish large enough to hold the fish. Brush the fish generously all over with the butter and place it in the dish, surrounded by the stuffing balls.

6. Cook in a preheated combination oven at 180°C with LOW power microwave for 16–20 minutes, basting halfway through. When the fish is done it will feel tender to the touch.

7. Lift the fish carefully on to a serving platter and garnish with the stuffing balls.

8. Finish the sauce by reheating on HIGH for 2 minutes. Stir in the cream. Pour a little of the sauce around the fish and serve the rest separately.

FRESH TUNA WITH MOSEL SAUCE

SERVES 4
•
4 tuna steaks

butter to grease dish

125 g (4 oz) button mushrooms, wiped and sliced

225 g (8 oz) tomatoes, skinned and chopped

15 ml (1 tbsp) chopped fresh parsley

salt and freshly ground black pepper

150 ml (5 fl oz) Mosel wine

150 ml (5 fl oz) double cream

Tuna is very common in the Mediterranean, but until recently, it was seldom seen in its fresh form in this country. It is however becoming more widely available and is well worth trying if you come across it. It is usually sold in steaks and is ideal for barbecuing in the summer as it is a ''meaty'' fish. If tuna is not available, try this recipe with whole mackerel which is a relative of tuna fish. As with most fish dishes, this is best served as soon as possible after cooking.

1. Place the steaks in a shallow, buttered dish. Sprinkle over the mushrooms, tomatoes, parsley, seasoning and wine. Cover and cook in a preheated combination oven at 180°C with LOW power microwave for 15–18 minutes, turning the steaks once during the cooking time.

2. Remove the steaks and keep warm on a serving dish. Remove the vegetables with a slotted spoon and arrange around the fish. Reduce the cooking liquor by microwaving on HIGH for 6 minutes.

3. Stir in the cream and microwave on HIGH for 2 minutes. Check the seasoning. Coat the tuna steaks with the sauce and serve at once.

FISH CURRY WITH CREAMED COCONUT

SERVES 4
•

25 g (1 oz) butter

1 clove garlic, crushed

1 small onion, finely chopped

15 ml (1 tbsp) plain flour

15 ml (1 tbsp) curry powder

grated rind and juice of ½ lemon

450 ml (¾ pt) hot fish stock (see page 39)

25 g (1 oz) sultanas

10 ml (2 tsp) tomato purée

30 ml (2 tbsp) sweet chutney

450 g (1 lb) haddock, skinned and chopped

salt and freshly ground black pepper

75 g (3 oz) creamed coconut

 This is a very quick curry, but it even impressed Malaysian friends of ours! The addition of the coconut was their idea, and adds authenticity to it. For a more elaborate dish, use 350 g (12 oz) peeled prawns in place of the haddock. This dish benefits from being made in advance and reheated.

1. Microwave the butter in a casserole dish on HIGH for 1 minute or until melted.

2. Stir in the garlic and onion and microwave on HIGH for 2 minutes.

3. Stir in the flour, curry powder, lemon rind and juice and fish stock. Microwave on HIGH for 3 minutes, stirring halfway through the cooking time.

4. Stir in the remaining ingredients, except for the coconut, cover and microwave on HIGH for 5 minutes, stirring occasionally.

5. Break up the coconut with a fork, then stir it into the curry. Leave to stand for a few minutes before serving with rice.

ANNALONG FISH PIE

SERVES 6
•
75 g (3 oz) butter

4 large lemon soles, skinned and filleted

15 ml (1 tbsp) lemon juice

5 sheets of filo pastry

Filling

300 ml (½ pt) fish stock (see Cook's tip)

50 g (2 oz) butter

50 g (2 oz) plain flour

salt and freshly ground black pepper

250 g (8 oz) monkfish, skinned and filleted

250 g (8 oz) shelled prawns

2 hard-boiled eggs, chopped

This pie was inspired by a visit to Annalong, a small fishing village nestling at the foot of the Mourne mountains in Northern Ireland. Here wonderful fresh fish can be obtained if you know the right people, and even if you do not, a short drive to Kilkeel with its fish market is a buyer's delight provided you don't mind buying large quantities. Make the pie with fresh fish if at all possible; not only is the flavour better but it is also less wet and the sauce will remain thick. If you wish reduce the stock and add some wine and cream although it is delicious enough without this refinement. Buy a few prawns in their shells for decoration. If the fish is fresh the pie can be made early in the day of serving. Make sure the sauce is cold before you add the fish to it, and top with the pastry. If frozen fish is used prepare it all but assemble the dish no more than an hour before cooking.

1. Using 25 g (1 oz) of the butter generously grease a 23 cm (9 in) square pie dish. Use half the fillets of sole to line the base of the dish. Sprinkle the lemon juice over the sole.

2. Make the filling: put the fish stock, butter and flour into a large jug or bowl and microwave on HIGH for 4 minutes, whisking well after each minute. Season well, and set aside.

3. Cut the monkfish into strips about the size of the prawns, and stir it into the sauce with the prawns and chopped hard-boiled eggs. The sauce should be very thick.

4. Pour the sauce over the sole and top with the remaining sole fillets.

5. Microwave the remaining butter in a small bowl on HIGH for 1 minute until melted. Cut the sheets of filo pastry in half. Working swiftly, brush each sheet of filo generously with melted butter. Layer the buttered sheets on top of the fish, making 9 layers in all. Cut the remaining half sheet of filo into fish and shell shapes to decorate the top of the pie. Trim the edges of the pie (do not tuck too much in) and brush the top generously with the remaining melted butter.

6. Cook in a preheated combination oven at 220°C with LOW power microwave for 12–15 minutes or until the crust is golden brown and crisp.

—— COOK'S TIP——

Use the skins and bones from the sole to make fish stock, following the method on page 39.

GRAVADLAX FISH LAYER

SERVES 4
•
675 g (1 ½ lb) potatoes

45 ml (3 tbsp) salted water

450 g (1 lb) cod fillet

5 ml (1 tsp) butter

175 g (6 oz) gravadlax

125 g (4 oz) Maasdan cheese, grated

200 ml (7 fl oz) double cream

salt and freshly ground black pepper

 Gravadlax is a Scandinavian pickled salmon. The fish is pickled with fresh dill, and is a delicious alternative to smoked salmon. It is now available in this country in delicatessens or – and this is how we get ours – can be purchased from a mail order company dealing mainly in smoked products. Gravadlax is not cheap, but it adds a very special touch to what otherwise would be a very simple dish. The result is delicious. Maasdan is a Dutch cheese with a nutty flavour similar to Emmenthal. Use Emmenthal as an alternative. To serve for a dinner party, prepare the dish in advance, but cook just before serving.

1. Peel the potatoes and cut into roughly 5 cm (2 in) chunks. Place in a casserole with the salted water, cover and microwave on HIGH for 8 minutes, turning the potatoes halfway through the cooking time. When cool enough to handle, slice the potatoes.

2. Skin the cod, and if it is a thick fillet, cut in half lengthways to form thinner fillets.

3. Grease a 25 × 20 cm (10 × 8 in) shallow dish with the butter. Arrange half the cod in the base of the dish. Cover the cod with half the gravadlax, then half the potatoes and half the cheese. Pour over half the cream and a little seasoning.

4. Repeat the layers with the remaining ingredients, ending with potato and cheese. Cook in a preheated combination oven at 200°C with LOW power microwave for 20 minutes. Serve at once.

MEAT, POULTRY AND GAME

*T*HIS CHAPTER INCLUDES a wide range of dishes aimed at using to their best advantage all the systems in your oven. With the combination oven system, succulent roasts can be cooked to carve at the table, while the microwave alone can be used for fast cooking of small tender portions of meat.

The recipes include many dishes which can be prepared well in advance of a dinner party: some may be made the previous day; others can be frozen. On the whole, those that require last-minute attention are not too fiddly.

Do remember to choose a main course that is going to complement the starter and dessert. Do not overface your guests with too much meat and remember the garnish.

RIB OF BEEF WITH MUSTARD SAUCE

SERVES 8
•
1 × 2 kg (4½ lb) rib of beef on the
bone

225 g (8 oz) mild whole-grain
mustard

150 ml (5 fl oz) double cream

 These days, it seems, a large joint of beef can only be justified if you are entertaining. It always creates quite a stir when brought to the table. In fact, a large joint is often more economical than a small one, particularly if it is on the bone, because it shrinks less. Rib of beef is a particularly good roast because the fat with which it is marbled makes it meltingly tender when cooked; a lean joint can never compete. If you are trying to cut down on the fat by all means avoid eating it, but don't cut it all off the joint before cooking.

This will really need to be cooked just before you bring your guests to the table. Tenting it under foil will help to keep it warm during the standing time. You may find it more convenient to make the sauce on the hob.

1. Coat the meat with 175 g (6 oz) of the mustard and place on a rack over a roasting dish.

2. Roast in a preheated combination oven at 170°C with LOW microwave for 14 minutes per 450 g (1 lb) (see Cook's tip) turning the meat over halfway through cooking. When the joint is cooked, rest the meat for 15 minutes before carving.

3. While the meat is resting make the sauce. Pour the meat juices into a dish, discarding some of the fat if necessary. Add the remaining mustard and the double cream (make sure you have less juice than cream) stir well, and microwave on HIGH until slightly reduced.

4. Carve the meat at the table and hand round the sauce separately.

—— COOK'S TIP——

The timing given above is for rare meat. If you prefer
beef a little better done, increase the timing to 17 minutes per
450 g (1 lb).

SPANISH BRISKET

SERVES 6–8
•
30 ml (2 tbsp) oil

1 medium onion, sliced

1 medium red pepper, seeded and sliced

1 medium green pepper, seeded and sliced

1 large leek, washed and sliced

15 ml (1 tbsp) tomato purée

150 ml (5 fl oz) red wine

1 kg (2¼ lb) joint of boned rolled brisket

50 g (2 oz) stuffed green olives, sliced

This is an economical dish, both in terms of time and money. It looks very bright and colourful and is ideal for all but the grandest dinner parties. You may like to serve it with jacket potatoes cooked alongside the casserole if your combination oven is big enough. They will only take about 40 minutes, so put them in once the meat has started cooking. The brisket can successfully be cooked in advance and sliced before reheating on the serving platter.

1. Combine the oil, onion, peppers and leek in a large deep casserole, cover and microwave on HIGH for 4 minutes.

2. Stir in the tomato purée and wine and bury the meat in the vegetables. Cover and cook in a preheated combination oven at 180°C with LOW power microwave for 1 hour–1 hour 10 minutes.

3. Stir the olives into the vegetable mixture, check the seasoning and leave to stand for 10 minutes for the flavour to develop.

4. Slice the meat and serve on a platter, surrounded by the vegetables.

MARINATED MINT AND ORANGE LAMB

SERVES 6–8
•

1 × 2 kg (4¼ lb) leg of lamb

30 ml (2 tbsp) wine vinegar

1 clove garlic, crushed

2 oranges

1 onion, roughly chopped

1 carrot, roughly chopped

1 bay leaf

900 ml (1½ pt) lamb stock

10 ml (2 tsp) arrowroot

fresh mint to garnish

Stuffing

25 g (1 oz) butter

1 onion, finely chopped

1 clove garlic, crushed

125 g (4 oz) fresh brown
breadcrumbs

15 ml (1 tbsp) chopped fresh mint

15 ml (1 tbsp) chopped fresh
parsley

grated rind and juice of ½ orange

salt and freshly ground black
pepper

1 egg

Coating

25 g (1 oz) fine white breadcrumbs

grated rind of ½ orange

salt and freshly ground black
pepper

This dish is best started the day before you want to serve it. Marinate the lamb overnight and make the lamb stock so that it can cool. Completing the dish will not take too much effort next day. The orange cuts through the fattiness of the lamb and the marinade makes it meltingly tender.

1. Bone the leg of lamb. Put the bones into a dish and roast in a preheated combination oven at 200°C with LOW power microwave for 30 minutes.

2. Meanwhile, trim the fat from the leg of lamb and place the joint in a glass dish with the vinegar and garlic. Peel 1 of the oranges in long strips, removing any pith. Cut the peel in julienne strips and set aside. Squeeze both oranges and add half the juice to the dish containing the lamb. Reserve the remaining orange juice. Marinate the lamb for up to 24 hours, turning occasionally.

3. Remove the roasted bones from the oven and place in a saucepan with the onion, carrot, bay leaf and stock. Bring to the boil on a conventional hob. Skim, lower the heat and simmer for 1 hour.

4. Strain the rich lamb stock into a clean saucepan and reduce by rapid boiling to 450 ml (¾ pt). Leave to cool, then refrigerate until required.

5. Next day make the stuffing: put the butter in a casserole with the onion and garlic. Microwave on HIGH for 4 minutes, stirring once. Add all the remaining stuffing ingredients and mix well.

6. Remove the lamb from the marinade and fill the leg cavity with the stuffing. Tie loosely to keep the leg shape. Mix all the ingredients for the coating together in a shallow bowl and turn the lamb in the mixture until well coated.

7. Weigh the joint and roast on a rack in a preheated combination oven at 200°C with LOW power microwave for 18 minutes per 450 g (1 lb), turning once. Leave the meat to stand for 20 minutes while you make the gravy.

8. Remove the fat from the chilled lamb stock and bring to the boil on a conventional hob. Mix the reserved orange juice with the arrowroot and stir into the boiling stock. Lower the heat and simmer until the gravy clears.

9. Place the reserved orange julienne in a bowl, add boiling water to cover and leave for 5 minutes. Drain and dry on paper towels.

10. Remove the string from the meat, place it on a serving dish and garnish with the fresh mint and orange julienne. Serve the gravy separately.

LOIN OF LAMB WITH RICE AND KIDNEY STUFFING

SERVES 8
•

150 g (5 oz) Italian risotto rice

350 ml (12 fl oz) boiling lamb stock (see Cook's tip)

1 onion, finely chopped

50 g (2 oz) butter

4 lambs' kidneys

15 ml (1 tbsp) chopped fresh mint

grated rind and juice of 1 orange

2 eggs

2 × 1.25 kg (2½ lb) untrimmed loins of lamb (trimmed weight about 1 kg/2¼ lb each)

Sauce

300 ml (½ pt) lamb stock

60 ml (4 tbsp) apple jelly

10 ml (2 tsp) arrowroot, mixed with 15 ml (1 tbsp) water

fresh mint to garnish

One complaint people seem to have about joints of meat is that they are difficult to carve. Well, this couldn't be easier; a nice neat sandwich of meat and stuffing. The rice makes it unusual and very tasty. Make up the stuffing and stuff the meat an hour or so before you intend to cook it. Once cooked, the meat will keep warm for about 20 minutes if tented under foil but don't forget to remove the string before serving!

1. Put the rice into a large deep casserole and add the stock (which must be boiling for accurate timing). Microwave on HIGH for 14 minutes, cover and leave to stand for 5 minutes, by which time all the liquid should have been absorbed and the rice should be tender. Set aside.

2. Put the onion in a bowl with the butter and microwave on HIGH for 2 minutes. Cut the kidneys into small pieces (this is easier to do if they are partly frozen). Add them to the onion, stir and microwave on HIGH for 4 minutes.

3. Stir in the mint, orange rind and juice, eggs and cooked rice. Pile on to one of the loins of lamb and place the second loin on top. You should end up with a fairly flat sandwich. Using a trussing needle and string, sew the two pieces of meat together at the edges.

4. Roast in a preheated combination oven at 190°C with LOW power microwave for 50 minutes. Then leave to stand for 10 minutes before carefully removing the string.

5. Make the sauce: Place the stock in a saucepan with the apple jelly. Bring to the boil on the hob, add the arrowroot mixture, reduce the heat and simmer until clear.

6. Serve the meat in thick slices, allowing 1 slice per person, garnish with mint and hand the sauce separately.

—— COOK'S TIP——

It is a good idea to make up the stock you will require well in advance, using the lamb bones and trimmings with a little extra help from a lamb stock cube. Cool the stock so you can remove any fat before using it.

APRICOT AND GINGER STUFFED LAMB FILLET

SERVES 6

•

4 fillets of lamb

1 small onion, finely chopped

50 g (2 oz) butter

50 g (2 oz) no-need-to-soak dried apricots, chopped

50 g (2 oz) walnuts, roughly chopped

50 g (2 oz) fresh brown breadcrumbs

15 ml (1 tbsp) chopped fresh parsley

5 cm (2 in) piece of fresh ginger, finely grated

1 egg

salt and freshly ground black pepper to taste

5 ml (1 tsp) ground ginger

30 ml (2 tbsp) runny honey

60 ml (4 tbsp) soy sauce

Lamb fillet is usually easy to get hold of during the spring but you may have to order it at other times of the year. The cooked lamb is pink which contrasts well with the orange of the apricots, and the crunchy walnuts create a contrast in texture. It is inclined to fall apart, which is why we suggest tying it well (if you don't want your guests to see the string we suggest you carve in the kitchen, arrange the slices on a serving plate and reheat if necessary). In spite of the slightly tricky serving this dish is absolutely delicious and well worth the effort.

1. Bat the meat out between sheets of greaseproof paper until it is flat, then trim off as much fat as possible. Marinate in soy sauce, if desired (see Cook's tip).

2. Put the onion and butter in a bowl and microwave on HIGH for 3 minutes. Add the apricots, walnuts, breadcrumbs, parsley, fresh ginger, egg and seasoning. Mix well.

3. Place 2 of the fillets on a work surface and top each with half the stuffing. Top with the remaining fillets. Fold the thin ends in if necessary. Tie each pair of fillets together using 6 pieces of string.

4. Rub the ground ginger over the meat and put into a shallow dish. Spread the fillets with honey and sprinkle with the soy sauce.

5. Roast in a preheated combination oven at 220°C with LOW power microwave for 20–25 minutes, turning over halfway through cooking.

6. Leave to stand for 10 minutes before carving into thick slices between each piece of string. Lay the slices on their sides so that the stuffing can be seen. Pour the cooking juices over and serve at once.

—— COOK'S TIP——

If you have time, sprinkle the lamb fillets with a little extra soy sauce and marinate for 1 hour or up to 1 day before stuffing.

CARIBBEAN PORK

SERVES 4

•

1 large onion, finely sliced

60 ml (4 tbsp) sunflower oil

450 g (1 lb) pork fillet, thinly sliced

1 cooking apple, peeled and finely chopped

5 ml (1 tsp) curry powder

10 ml (2 tsp) paprika

½ banana, peeled and sliced

10 ml (2 tsp) cornflour

150 ml (5 fl oz) white wine

150 ml (5 fl oz) double cream

salt to taste

Garnish

1 banana, sliced

15 ml (1 tbsp) lemon juice

15 ml (1 tbsp) chopped fresh parsley

This recipe may sound a little odd but it certainly doesn't taste it! It can be cooked in advance and reheated to serve. Be sure to cover the top with a layer of damp greaseproof paper to prevent the formation of a skin if there is going to be any delay before serving. Brown rice and crunchy green beans make ideal accompaniments.

1. Mix the onion and oil in a large casserole and microwave on HIGH for 3–4 minutes.

2. Add the pork, apple, curry powder and paprika to the casserole, stir well and cover. Microwave on HIGH for 6 minutes. Add the banana.

3. Mix the cornflour with a little of the wine and stir it into the pork mixture, with the remaining wine and the cream.

4. Microwave on HIGH for a further 7 minutes, stirring once or twice. Season to taste.

5. Garnish with the banana (dipped in lemon juice to avoid discoloration) and top with the parsley.

PORK OLIVES

SERVES 4

•

4 pork escalopes (total weight 575 g/1¼ lb)

30 ml (2 tbsp) oil

1 onion, chopped

1 carrot, peeled and sliced

250 ml (8 fl oz) white wine

30 ml (2 tbsp) tomato purée

5 ml (1 tsp) arrowroot

15 ml (1 tbsp) water

Stuffing

50 g (2 oz) mushrooms, wiped and chopped

125 g (4 oz) minced pork

15 ml (1 tbsp) Parmesan cheese

25 g (1 oz) fresh breadcrumbs

15 ml (1 tbsp) chopped fresh parsley

5 ml (1 tsp) sage

salt and freshly ground black pepper

1 egg

We always like recipes which are ready portioned: not only are they easy to serve, but there is also no worry about there being enough to go round. These are so delicious, however, that you may need to make extra for second helpings! To prepare for a dinner party, we suggest that you make the "olives" in the afternoon, brown them and then place in a casserole with the sauce ingredients. Keep cool, then cook as described in step 3 to serve.

1. Place the escalopes between 2 sheets of dampened greaseproof paper and flatten with a rolling pin. Cut each in half.

2. Mix together all the stuffing ingredients, binding with the egg. Spread over the escalopes, then roll each one up and secure with a wooden cocktail stick.

3. Heat the oil in a frying pan on a conventional hob, brown the escalopes quickly, then place them in a casserole. Add the onion, carrot, wine and tomato purée. Cover and cook in a preheated combination oven at 180°C with LOW power microwave for 25 minutes.

4. Remove the escalopes, and keep warm on a serving dish. Strain the sauce, returning the liquid to the casserole. Blend the arrowroot with the water, add to the sauce and microwave on HIGH for 2 minutes.

5. Remove the cocktail sticks from the escalopes, pour the sauce over and serve at once.

GAMMON IN CUMBERLAND SAUCE

This very easy dinner party dish looks superb with its rich ruby-coloured sauce. Gammon slices can be very expensive and are sometimes too large for delicate appetites: a useful tip, therefore, is to buy a gammon joint and slice it yourself. For a crisper effect, the gammon can be grilled instead of cooked in the microwave. The dish does not freeze, but can be prepared in advance for a dinner party and just reheated, covered, at the last minute.

SERVES 4

•

4 slices gammon

15 g (½ oz) butter

300 ml (½ pt) red wine

60 ml (4 tbsp) redcurrant jelly

grated rind and juice of 1 lemon

grated rind and juice of 1 orange

125 g (4 oz) button mushrooms, wiped and sliced

15 ml (1 tbsp) arrowroot

30 ml (2 tbsp) water

1. Place the gammon slices in a large shallow dish, dot with butter and cover. Microwave on HIGH for 8–10 minutes.

2. Combine all the remaining ingredients except the arrowroot and water in a large measuring jug. Stir thoroughly, then microwave on HIGH for 5 minutes, stirring halfway through the cooking time.

3. Mix the arrowroot with the water and stir into the sauce. Microwave on HIGH for 2 minutes. Serve the gammon coated with a little of the sauce, putting the remainder in a sauce boat.

JAMBON À LA CRÈME

This potentially rich dish is lightened by the fresh chopped tomatoes and the result is delicious. By using the combination oven, the gammon needs no pre-cooking. We made the sauce on the hob while the oven was preheating.

SERVES 4

•

4 gammon slices

25 g (1 oz) butter

1 small onion, finely chopped

125 g (4 oz) button mushrooms, wiped and sliced

25 g (1 oz) plain flour

150 ml (5 fl oz) dry white wine

150 ml (5 fl oz) double cream

450 g (1 lb) tomatoes, skinned and chopped

salt and freshly ground black pepper

1. Place the gammon in a large shallow dish.

2. Melt the butter in a saucepan on a conventional hob and sauté the onion and mushrooms until softened. Stir in the flour and cook for 1 minute. Gradually blend in the wine, then stir in the cream and bring to the boil. Stir in the tomatoes and season to taste, being sparing with the salt.

3. Pour the sauce over the gammon and cook in a preheated combination oven at 180°C, with LOW power microwave for 20 minutes.

4. Serve the gammon at once with buttered noodles and either fresh vegetables or a crisp salad.

FESTIVAL CHICKEN WITH CHOCOLATE, RAISINS AND PINE KERNELS

SERVES 8
•
1 × 2 kg (4–5 lb) roasting chicken

salt and freshly ground black pepper

a little cinnamon

Stuffing

225 g (8 oz) minced beef

40 g (1 ½ oz) plain chocolate

300 ml (½ pt) beef stock

150 g (5 oz) raisins

50 g (2 oz) pine kernels

2.5 ml (½ tsp) ground cloves

5 ml (1 tsp) ground coriander

5 ml (1 tsp) ground cinnamon

150 ml (5 fl oz) red wine

This is a very unusual chicken dish. The recipe originated in Mexico where it is used to celebrate festivals. The contrast of colours is wonderful – black and white – and in spite of the recipe sounding rather odd it has proved popular on courses at the Contemporary Cookery School. It goes very well with a combination of buttered spinach with 5 ml (1 tsp) nutmeg and 50 g (2 oz) toasted pine kernels. When serving this for a dinner party it would be easiest to make the stuffing in advance. Do not stuff the bird until just before you are going to cook it.

1. Combine all the stuffing ingredients in a saucepan on a conventional hob. Bring to the boil, lower the heat and simmer until the mixture is thick and most of the liquid has evaporated; this will take about 20 minutes.

2. When the stuffing is cool use it to stuff the breast cavity of the chicken, being sure to truss the bird well, so that the stuffing does not leak during cooking. Place the bird in a roasting pan and season with the salt and pepper and a little cinnamon.

3. Cook in a preheated combination oven at 190°C with LOW power microwave for 1 hour or until the legs move easily and juices that run when a knife is inserted between the thigh and breast are clear. Baste occasionally.

4. Leave to rest for 10 minutes before carving, and serve with a sauce made from the pan juices.

LEMONY CHICKEN WITH GARLIC AND GINGER

SERVES 4
•
4 chicken breasts

1 lemon

50 g (2 oz) spring onions, finely chopped

2 cloves garlic, crushed

2.5 cm (1 in) piece of fresh ginger, peeled and grated

450 ml (¾ pt) good chicken stock

175 g (6 oz) fromage frais

salt and freshly ground black pepper

additional spring onions, sliced diagonally, to garnish

 When most of us entertain, we tend to turn to recipes that are either extravagant or indulgent. Here for a change is a recipe that is low in saturated fat and yet still tastes rich. The chicken is wonderfully tender and the dish looks good too. If you wish, serve the chicken sliced and arranged on individual plates but this has to be done at the last minute; fine for a restaurant with plenty of staff but just more work for a solo cook. Start this dish the evening before you need it. On the day reduce the stock and at the last minute make the sauce and cook the chicken.

1. Skin and bone the chicken breasts. Cut half the rind of the lemon into julienne strips; grate the remainder.

2. Combine the spring onions, garlic, grated lemon rind and ginger in a blender or food processor and work to a smooth paste, adding a little water if necessary.

3. Spread the paste over the chicken. Cover well and marinate for at least 2 hours or up to 24 hours.

4. Scrape the paste from the chicken and place in a saucepan on a conventional hob. Add the stock. Bring to the boil, then lower the heat and simmer for 15 minutes.

5. Strain the stock into a clean saucepan and reduce by fast boiling to 50 ml (2 fl oz); pour the reduced stock into a large measuring jug and set aside.

6. Arrange the chicken breasts in a shallow dish. Cover and microwave on HIGH for 8 minutes repositioning them once during the cooking time.

7. Gradually whisk the fromage frais into the reduced stock in the jug until smooth. Microwave on MEDIUM for 4 minutes whisking every minute or until hot. Do not allow the sauce to boil.

8. Place the reserved lemon julienne in a bowl with water to cover. Microwave on HIGH for 2 minutes, drain and dry on paper towels.

9. Serve the chicken breasts with a little of the sauce poured over. Garnish with the lemon strips and sliced spring onions, and hand the remaining sauce separately.

CHICKEN AMARETTO

SERVES 4

•

4 chicken breasts, skinned

125 g (4 oz) seedless green grapes, halved

50 g (2 oz) Gouda cheese, grated

seasoned flour

25 g (1 oz) butter

4 medium-sized lettuce leaves

30 ml (2 tbsp) Amaretto di Saronno

60 ml (4 tbsp) chicken stock

150 ml (5 fl oz) double cream

salt and freshly ground black pepper

To Garnish

25 g (1 oz) toasted, flaked almonds

chopped fresh parsley

 This is an adaptation of a recipe once made by the chef of the Hyde Park Hotel, so it has a good pedigree! Amaretto is a delicious Italian almond liqueur which goes particularly well with chicken, but should also be tried in a variety of desserts. This recipe does not "sit" particularly well, especially once the lettuce leaves are added. The most time-consuming part is stuffing the chicken breasts. This can be done in advance and the dish cooked at the last minute. Try to buy chicken supremes which still have the little wing bone attached. This holds the chicken together.

1. Place a chicken breast on a board, then carefully lift off the fillet. Cover the fillet with damp greaseproof paper then flatten carefully with a meat mallet and place on one side.

2. With a sharp knife, make a lengthways incision in the centre of the breast, taking care neither to cut right through it nor to extend the incision to the edges. Now make 2 incisions at right angles to the first and on either side of it, effectively creating two flaps which can be folded back to reveal a pocket. Place some of the grapes in the pocket, cover with a quarter of the grated cheese and add some more of the grapes. Place the flattened fillet over the filling and fold the flaps over to reshape the breast. Repeat with the remaining chicken breasts. Coat the breasts in seasoned flour.

3. Microwave the butter in a shallow dish on HIGH for 1 minute or until melted. Turn the breasts over in the butter, then cover and cook in a preheated combination oven at 180°C with LOW power microwave for 20 minutes, turning over halfway through the cooking time.

4. Meanwhile blanch the lettuce leaves in boiling water for a few seconds then drain.

5. With a slotted spoon, lift the chicken breasts from the dish and wrap each one in a lettuce leaf. Place on a serving dish and keep warm. Add the Amaretto, stock and cream to the butter remaining in the dish and microwave on HIGH for about 7 minutes or until thickened. Season to taste.

6. Pour the sauce over the chicken, garnish with the toasted almonds and chopped parsley and serve at once.

CHICKEN WITH ROQUEFORT IN FILO PASTRY

SERVES 4
•
4 chicken breasts, skinned

125 g (4 oz) Roquefort cheese

50 g (2 oz) butter

4 double sheets filo pastry

A simple but delicious idea, sealed in a crisp filo parcel. The sharp flavour of the cheese goes particularly well with the chicken breasts. The parcels may be prepared in advance, brushed with melted butter, then chilled in the refrigerator. Cook the parcels at the last minute and serve at once.

1. Make a pocket in each chicken breast, following the instructions in steps 1 and 2 of the recipe for Chicken Amaretto (opposite page).

2. Divide the cheese into 4, and use to stuff the pockets. Place the flattened chicken fillets over the cheese and fold the flaps over to reshape the breasts.

3. In a small bowl, microwave the butter on HIGH for 1 minute until melted.

4. Open out the sheets of filo pastry, brush generously with butter, then fold in half to form a square. Brush again with butter.

5. Place a chicken breast on a corner of each filo pastry square and roll up, folding in the edges to form a neat parcel. Repeat with remaining chicken breasts.

6. Arrange the chicken on a baking dish, brush with the remaining butter and bake in a preheated combination oven at 200°C with LOW power microwave for 15 minutes.

CASSEROLE OF DUCK IN CIDER

SERVES 4
•
1 duck, jointed into 4, or 4 duck pieces

225 g (8 oz) tomatoes, skinned and roughly chopped

225 g (8 oz) carrots, peeled and sliced

5 ml (1 tsp) thyme

120 ml (4 fl oz) fresh orange juice

175 ml (6 fl oz) medium sweet cider

10 ml (2 tsp) cornflour

15 ml (1 tbsp) water

10 ml (2 tsp) tomato purée

salt and freshly ground black pepper

 We developed this recipe to use the leg joints from 2 ducks, having used the breasts in another dish (Alassio duck, below). However, 1 whole duck can be used, jointed into 4, or even the frozen duck joints that are now widely available from freezer centres. We skinned the joints and removed any excess fat. This recipe can be prepared to the oven-ready stage in advance.

1. Skin the duck and remove any extra fat.

2. Place the tomatoes and carrots in a casserole and lay the duck joints on top.

3. Mix the thyme, orange juice and cider in a bowl and pour over the duck. Cover and cook in a preheated combination oven at 180°C with LOW power microwave for 45 minutes, or until the juices in the duck run clear.

4. Blend the cornflour with the water, then stir into the casserole with the tomato purée. Season to taste, then microwave on HIGH for 2 minutes before serving, with savoury rice, if liked.

ALASSIO DUCK

SERVES 4
•
4 duck breasts

15 g (½ oz) butter

15 ml (1 tbsp) finely chopped onion

50 ml (2 fl oz) dry vermouth

20 ml (4 tsp) green peppercorns

150 ml (5 fl oz) double cream

salt

Duck can often be rich and rather fatty, but in this recipe only the skinned breasts are used and the fat removed. Duck breasts can be bought on the bone frozen in pairs. Otherwise, a good idea is to order 2 whole ducks from the butcher, jointed. Use the breasts for this recipe and freeze the leg joints to use at a later date for Casserole of duck in cider (above). To cook Alassio duck for a dinner party, complete step 1 and 2 in advance, then finish the recipe at the last minute.

1. Bone the breasts, if necessary, and remove the skin and any fat. Microwave the butter in a shallow casserole on HIGH for 30 seconds or until melted. Stir in the onion, add the duck breasts and turn over in the butter.

2. Pour in the vermouth, cover and cook in a preheated combination oven at 200°C, with LOW power microwave for 20–25 minutes or until the duck is cooked through.

3. With a slotted spoon, transfer the duck breasts to a warm serving dish. Add the peppercorns and cream to the dish in which the duck was cooked. Microwave on HIGH for 5 minutes or until slightly thickened. Add salt to taste, pour over the duck and serve.

TURKEY FILLETS WITH FRESH SAGE

SERVES 4

•

4 turkey fillets

seasoned flour

15 g (½ oz) butter

15 ml (1 tbsp) olive oil

125 g (4 oz) gammon, cut into thin strips

150 ml (5 fl oz) white wine

150 ml (5 fl oz) chicken stock

15 ml (1 tbsp) chopped fresh sage

5 ml (1 tsp) cornflour

15 ml (1 tbsp) water

salt and white pepper

fresh sage leaves to garnish

Turkey is a very economical meat, even the tender fillets being inexpensive. It can, however be somewhat lacking in flavour, so other ingredients need to be carefully chosen. This is a very simple recipe, but delicious in both flavour and aroma. Your guests will be seated with mouths watering as the delightful smell of fresh sage permeates the dining room. Dried sage can be used, but is a poor substitute for the real thing. This recipe reheats successfully, so can be made in advance.

1. Cut each turkey fillet in half, then coat in seasoned flour. Place the butter and oil in a large shallow dish and microwave on HIGH for 1 minute. Turn the turkey over in the butter, then cook in a preheated combination oven at 180°C with LOW power microwave for 10 minutes.

2. Turn the turkey fillets over, add the gammon and continue cooking at 180°C with LOW power microwave for 5 minutes more.

3. Pour over the wine, stock and chopped sage, cover and continue to combination cook at 180°C with LOW power microwave for 15 minutes.

4. With a slotted spoon, remove the turkey and keep warm. Turn off the combination oven controls, then replace the sauce in the oven and boil on HIGH power microwave for 8 minutes.

5. Blend the cornflour with the water, stir into the sauce and cook on HIGH for 2 minutes. Season to taste, pour the sauce over the turkey and serve garnished with sage leaves.

SALMI OF PHEASANT

SERVES 6
•

1 brace of pheasants

12 smoked streaky bacon rashers

25 g (1 oz) butter

15 ml (1 tbsp) olive oil

1 carrot, peeled and chopped

1 small onion, chopped

2 sticks celery, chopped

175 g (6 oz) button mushrooms

15 ml (1 tbsp) plain flour

*450 ml (¾ pt) hot pheasant stock
(see Cook's tip)*

10 ml (2 tsp) tomato purée

bay leaf

2 parsley stalks

150 ml (5 fl oz) port

30 ml (2 tbsp) redcurrant jelly

*salt and freshly ground black
pepper*

Although pheasant is delicious simply roasted with all the trimmings, this recipe based on a traditional salmi should definitely be tried. A "salmi" is a type of stew using roast game which is then jointed and cooked in a wine sauce. This recipe can easily be adapted for other game. To serve for a dinner party, prepare in advance and simply reheat to serve.

1. Pluck and draw the pheasants, then wipe out the cavities. Place the birds in a roasting dish, cover with 8 of the bacon rashers and roast in a preheated combination oven at 200°C with LOW power microwave for 30–35 minutes.

2. When the pheasants are cool enough to handle, joint each into 4 by removing the breasts, then cutting off the legs with the remaining meat. Remove the skin, place the joints in a shallow casserole and set aside.

3. Place the butter in a large bowl and microwave on HIGH for 1 minute until melted. Add the oil, carrot, onion and celery. Chop the remaining bacon and add, together with the chopped mushroom stalks (slice the caps and reserve). Mix well, cover and microwave on HIGH for 10 minutes.

4. Stir in the flour, then gradually blend in the stock and tomato purée. Microwave on HIGH for 5 minutes, then add the bay leaf and parsley and microwave on LOW for 15 minutes.

5. Strain the sauce into a jug. Stir in the port, redcurrant jelly and reserved sliced mushrooms, then pour over the pheasant. Return to the oven and microwave on HIGH for 8 minutes or until the pheasant is hot. Season and serve.

—— COOK'S TIP——

When jointing the pheasant, reserve the breast bones and use to make a stock, following the instructions given in steps 1 and 3 of Marinated mint and orange lamb (see page 52) and using water as the liquid.

SADDLE OF HARE WITH JUNIPER SAUCE

SERVES 3–4

•

1 saddle of hare

150 ml (5 fl oz) port

juice of ½ lemon

5 ml (1 tsp) thyme

15 ml (1 tbsp) juniper berries, crushed

freshly ground black pepper

125 g (4 oz) smoked streaky bacon, rind removed

10 ml (2 tsp) plain flour

150 ml (5 fl oz) stock made from neck of hare

salt

 Many people may see this recipe and pass it by, but stop and read! The result is delicious. Hare is a very inexpensive, but underused game meat. It is only available from August to the end of February, and usually needs to be ordered from the butcher. It does, however, freeze well, so it is worthwhile buying on impulse and freezing for use at a later date. Freeze the saddle and neck separately, so that 2 meals can be made. Stewed or jugged hare is the most common serving method, so a recipe for roast hare is a delightful surprise. Ask your butcher to joint the hare for you, leaving the saddle whole and removing the legs (save these for Hare Bourguignonne, see page 66). The saddle of hare is best marinated overnight and the stock prepared in advance. It is then a simple last-minute task to roast and prepare the sauce.

1. Discard the thin membrane covering the saddle, then place in a shallow dish. Mix together the port, lemon juice, thyme, juniper berries and black pepper. Pour over the meat and marinate for 4 hours or overnight.

2. Drain the saddle, reserving the marinade, and place in a roasting dish. Cover with the streaky bacon. Roast in a preheated combination oven at 200°C with LOW power microwave for 30 minutes.

3. With slotted spoons, remove the hare and keep warm. Do the same with the crisp bacon. Drain the cooking liquor into a small saucepan on a conventional hob. Stir in the flour, cook for 1 minute, then gradually blend in the stock and reserved marinade. Bring to the boil, then add salt to taste.

4. To serve the hare, remove the fillets from the bone and slice thinly. Serve coated with sauce and accompanied by the crisp bacon. Game chips (see page 81) may also be served.

HARE BOURGUIGNONNE

SERVES 6–8
•

50 g (2 oz) butter

15 ml (1 tbsp) olive oil

1 hare, jointed

1 onion, sliced

2 cloves garlic, crushed

15 ml (1 tbsp) plain flour

45 ml (3 tbsp) brandy

bouquet garni

600 ml (1 pt) red wine

125 g (4 oz) smoked streaky bacon rashers, chopped

16 shallots, peeled

125 g (4 oz) button mushrooms, wiped and trimmed

salt and freshly ground black pepper

chopped fresh parsley

 This adaptation of the traditional Boeuf Bourguignonne recipe works very well for hare. This recipe was originally developed to use up the leftover joints of hare after the saddle has been roasted in another recipe (Saddle of hare with juniper sauce, page 65). In this way two completely different recipes were achieved from a single hare, but this works equally well with the joints from a whole hare. As with most casseroles, this benefits from cooking the day before.

1. Melt 25 g (1 oz) of the butter with the oil in a large frying pan on a conventional hob. Quickly brown the hare joints, add the onion and garlic and cook gently until transparent.

2. Stir in the flour and cook for 1 minute, then warm the brandy, pour over the hare and set alight.

3. When the flames have died down, empty the frying pan into a casserole. Add the bouquet garni, then pour over the red wine. Cover and cook in a pre-heated combination oven at 180°C with LOW power microwave for 30 minutes.

4. Meanwhile, melt the remaining butter in the frying pan and fry the bacon and shallots until the bacon is crisp and the shallots golden. Tip the onions and bacon into the casserole, cover and return to the combination oven at 180°C with LOW power microwave for 10 minutes.

5. Stir in the mushrooms and return to the combination oven at 180°C with LOW power microwave for a further 5 minutes. Season to taste, sprinkle with chopped parsley and serve at once, with Game chips (see page 81 and Savoy in orange butter (see page 76) if liked.

ROAST HAUNCH OF VENISON WITH SOUR CREAM SAUCE

SERVES 8
•

1.5 kg (1 lb) haunch of venison

4 back bacon rashers

150 ml (5 fl oz) beef stock

15 ml (1 tbsp) cornflour

30 ml (2 tbsp) water

15 ml (1 tbsp) mustard

150 ml (5 fl oz) sour cream

salt

Marinade

300 ml (½ pt) red wine

1 onion, chopped

1 carrot, peeled and chopped

30 ml (2 tbsp) oil

30 ml (2 tbsp) wine vinegar

6 peppercorns

bouquet garni

This is a meat which will become more and more widely available during the next few years. At the moment a good game butcher will stock venison or it may often be ordered. It is worth buying when available and storing in the freezer. At first glance you may think the meat is expensive, but as there is no wastage and it is so rich, a little goes a long way. The following recipe served 9 at a recent dinner party. Do allow plenty of time for the meat to marinade – it needs a minimum of 2 days and then the result will be as tender as fillet steak. The amount of vinegar makes a very piquant sauce; for a milder flavour use only 15 ml (1 tbsp).

1. Place the venison in a shallow dish. Mix all the marinade ingredients together and pour over the meat. Cover and leave in a cool place for 2 days, basting and turning over occasionally.

2. Remove the meat from the marinade and dry with paper towels. Reserve the marinade. Place the meat in a roasting dish, cover with bacon, then cover with a lid. Roast in a preheated combination oven at 200°C with LOW power microwave for 30 minutes. Remove the lid, then continue cooking for a further 20 minutes.

3. To make the sauce, strain the marinade into a saucepan. Add the stock and any juices from the meat. Bring to the boil on the conventional hob.

4. Mix the cornflour with the water and stir into the sauce. Bring back to the boil and stir until thickened. Stir in the mustard and cream and reheat but do not boil. Season with a little salt to taste.

5. Serve the venison with crispy bacon accompanied by the sauce, fresh vegetables, and Game chips (see page 81) if liked.

VEGETABLES AND VEGETARIAN DISHES

*T*HE MICROWAVE IS justly famous for the way it cooks vegetables. They stay crisp and bright in colour. It must be said, though, that cooking vegetables in the microwave is often no quicker than cooking by traditional methods, but because very little water is needed the nutritional value is retained. Another very great advantage, particularly if you are entertaining is that you can often cook the vegetables in the dish in which they are to be served, which means one less thing to wash up!

A trip to a large supermarket or greengrocer reveals that the number of varieties of vegetable easily obtained has expanded. We have included some recipes for the more unusual vegetables as well as new ways with the old familiar ones.

With vegetarians in view, we have included some more substantial recipes which even meat-eaters will enjoy.

Vegetables have a bigger place in our diet than ever before and beautiful fresh vegetables cooked well and served with something simple can really make a meal memorable.

OPPOSITE
Stuffed red fish with spinach sauce (page 44) with Spiced potato sticks (page 80);
Lemon and primrose gratin (page 89).

OVERLEAF
Spiced citrus sunflower (page 24); Lemony chicken with garlic and ginger (page 59) and
Casseroled new potatoes with garlic (page 79); Pear and caramel Bavarois (page 90)
with Tuiles (page 92).

FRENCH BEANS WITH CASHEW NUTS

SERVES 4

•

25 g (1 oz) unsalted cashew nuts

1 clove garlic, crushed

25 g (1 oz) butter

*350 g (12 oz) French beans,
trimmed*

Green beans are a popular vegetable: they can be eaten hot or cold, so leftovers never go to waste. They also stand very well and reheat perfectly. This makes them ideal for dinner parties. For this recipe always add the nuts at the last minute so that they don't lose their crispness. The combination of garlic, nuts and beans is irresistible.

1. Put the nuts on a plate and microwave on HIGH for 4 minutes or until toasted, turning occasionally.

2. Place the garlic in a casserole with the butter, cover and microwave on HIGH for 2 minutes.

3. Cut the beans into 4 cm (1½ in) lengths. Stir them into the garlic butter and cover. Microwave on HIGH for 6 minutes, stir and test – they may need another minute. The beans should remain crisp.

4. Scatter the nuts over the beans just before serving.

PREVIOUS PAGE
Indian menu à la carte (pages 122–124); From left to right clockwise: Poppadoms;
Mung dahl; rice; Kachoombar; Tandoori scampi and Saag gosht.

OPPOSITE
Christmas Dinner (pages 150–153); Roast goose with two stuffings; Brussels sprouts
with chestnuts; Carrot sticks with lemon and cardamom; Frozen ginger meringue
pudding with chocolate holly leaves; Mincemeat handkerchiefs.

CREAMED MUSHROOMS WITH PARSLEY AND GARLIC

SERVES 4
•
1 clove garlic, crushed

1 small onion, finely chopped

25 g (1 oz) butter

225 g (8 oz) button mushrooms, wiped

30 ml (2 tbsp) chopped fresh parsley

30 ml (2 tbsp) double cream

freshly grated nutmeg to taste

salt and freshly ground black pepper

This vegetable goes particularly well with beef. Be lavish with the mushrooms, as they shrink so much. If you wish to serve more guests you will not need to double up on all the ingredients, just the mushrooms. Cook the onion and garlic in advance if you wish and have all the other ingredients ready. If the onion mixture is cold you will need to increase the time in stage 2 to 5 minutes.

1. Combine the garlic, onion and butter in a bowl. Microwave on HIGH for 3 minutes, stirring once. Add the mushrooms, stirring well. Microwave uncovered on HIGH for 4 minutes.

2. Stir in the remaining ingredients and microwave uncovered on HIGH for 1 minute more. Serve at once.

CELERY AU GRATIN

SERVES 4
•
1 head of celery

1 × 213 g (7 oz) can tomatoes

15 ml (1 tbsp) grated onion

2.5 ml (½ tsp) dried thyme

freshly ground black pepper

25 g (1 oz) fresh breadcrumbs

25 g (1 oz) Cheddar cheese, grated

Cooked celery is inclined to be a bit watery; cook it like this and the problem will be avoided. The white and red of this dish contrast well to make it a colourful accompaniment. If you want to serve this as a vegetarian dish increase the quantity of cheese on the top. Prepare the dish in advance but cook it at the last minute.

1. Wash the celery and cut into 2.5 cm (1 in) lengths.

2. Drain the can of tomatoes, reserving the juice for use in another dish. Break up the tomatoes and put them into a gratin dish with the celery, onion, thyme and pepper.

3. Mix the breadcrumbs and cheese together and spinkle over the celery mixture.

4. Bake in a preheated combination oven at 200°C with MEDIUM power microwave for 15–20 minutes or until the top is crisp and the celery is tender.

FENNEL PARMESAN

SERVES 4
•
50 g (2 oz) butter

450 g (1 lb) fennel bulbs

50 g (2 oz) grated Parmesan cheese

salt and freshly ground black pepper

 This is a deliciously different vegetable dish, which slightly caramelises when cooked in the combination oven. It can successfully be cooked in advance and reheated at the last moment. Fennel complements fish particularly well.

1. Using 5 ml (1 tsp) of the butter, grease a casserole.

2. Slice the fennel. Layer it in the casserole with the Parmesan, finishing with a layer of Parmesan. Dot with the remaining butter.

3. Season sparingly with salt but generously with pepper. Cover.

4. Cook in a preheated combination oven at 180°C with LOW power microwave for 30 minutes. Serve at once.

CASSEROLED JERUSALEM ARTICHOKES WITH TOMATO AND ONION

SERVES 4
•
1 onion, chopped

30 ml (2 tbsp) olive oil

450 g (1 lb) Jerusalem artichokes

225 g (8 oz) tomatoes

2.5 ml (½ tsp) marjoram

salt and freshly ground black pepper

 Artichokes make an excellent alternative to potatoes. They are lower in calories, too. This nutritious dish is fairly moist and would be best served with a plain firm green vegetable such as French beans, and a meat dish such as roast lamb.

1. Place the onion in a casserole with the olive oil. Microwave on HIGH for 3 minutes.

2. Scrub the artichokes and add them to the casserole.

3. Skin the tomatoes by pouring boiling water over them and leaving for 1 minute; the skin should peel off easily. Quarter the tomatoes and discard the seeds. Add the flesh to the casserole with the marjoram and a little seasoning.

4. Bake in a preheated combination oven at 200°C with LOW power microwave for 35–40 minutes or until tender.

5. Stir well and check the seasoning before serving.

BUTTERED CUCUMBER WITH TARRAGON

SERVES 6
•
1 large cucumber, cut in 5 × 1 cm (2 × ½ in) sticks

5 ml (1 tsp) dried tarragon

50 g (2 oz) butter

5 ml (1 tsp) plain flour

salt and freshly ground black pepper

fresh tarragon to garnish (optional)

 Cucumber is a delicately flavoured vegetable, very unusual and best served with something light like chicken or fish. Do not cook this in advance because it will become too wet. The cucumber sticks can, however, be prepared several days ahead if kept in a plastic bag in the salad compartment of a refrigerator.

1. Combine the cucumber and tarragon in a dish, cover and microwave on HIGH for 4 minutes.

2. Drain and stir in the butter then the flour. Microwave on HIGH for 2 minutes.

3. Stir, season to taste and return to the microwave for a further minute.

4. Serve garnished with a sprig of fresh tarragon if available.

SAVOY IN ORANGE BUTTER

SERVES 4–6
•
1 × 275 g (10 oz) Savoy cabbage (approximate weight)

25 g (1 oz) butter

grated rind of 1 orange

freshly ground black pepper

 Of all the cabbages, the Savoy has to be the best. The beautifully patterned leaves with their varying shades of green give interest and texture to the vegetable and when cooked in the microwave the colour and flavour are excellent. The orange butter sweetens the cabbage and goes particularly well with game dishes.

1. Cut the cabbage into quarters. Cut away and discard the thickest part of the stalk, then shred. Rinse the shredded cabbage in water then shake dry in a colander.

2. Microwave the butter in a casserole on HIGH for 1 minute. Stir in the orange rind and cabbage. Season with plenty of black pepper.

3. Microwave the cabbage on HIGH for 3 minutes, stirring halfway through the cooking time. Serve at once.

GLAZED TURNIPS

SERVES 6

•

75 g (3 oz) unsalted butter

50 g (2 oz) demerara sugar

900 g (2 lb) turnips, peeled but left whole

 The much maligned turnip becomes a gourmet-style vegetable with this simple but unusual way of serving. Hand pick tiny turnips about the size of a tangerine for this recipe. To cook for a dinner party, either melt the butter and sugar, coat the turnips and put into the oven at the last minute or cook completely and keep warm in an open dish in a conventional oven.

1. Microwave the butter in a roasting dish on HIGH for 2 minutes until melted. Stir in the sugar and microwave on HIGH for 2 minutes more.

2. Turn the turnips over in the butter, then cook in a preheated combination oven at 200°C with LOW power microwave for 20 minutes or until tender and brown, turning occasionally. Serve at once.

BEETROOT WITH WHITE SAUCE

SERVES 4

•

4 medium raw beetroot (total weight about 450 g/1 lb)

30 ml (2 tbsp) water

25 g (1 oz) margarine or butter

25 ml (1 oz) plain flour

300 ml (½ pt) milk

salt and freshly ground black pepper

 Freshly cooked beetroot is delicious served hot as a vegetable. It cooks very well in the microwave, and can be served either sliced or whole if ''baby'' vegetables are used. If preparing in advance, cook the beetroot and sauce separately, then cool, placing a piece of greaseproof paper over the sauce to prevent the formation of a skin. Then reheat both and combine at the last minute.

1. Wash the beetroot and tear off the leaves, leaving a little of the stalk. Pierce the skin with a fork in several places.

2. Place in a casserole with the water, cover and microwave on HIGH for about 16 minutes. Rearrange the beetroot several times during cooking.

3. When cool enough to handle, peel and slice the beetroot and arrange in a serving dish.

4. Microwave the butter in a jug on HIGH for 1 minute, until melted. Stir in the flour, then gradually beat in the milk. Microwave on HIGH for 2 minutes, whisk thoroughly, then microwave on HIGH for 2 minutes more.

5. Whisk again, season to taste, then pour over the beetroot.

COURGETTE, CARROT AND PARSNIP SHREDS

SERVES 4–6

•

225 g (8 oz) courgettes

225 g (8 oz) carrots

225 g (8 oz) parsnips

25 g (1 oz) butter

2.5 ml (½ tsp) sugar

salt and freshly ground black pepper

This is a colourful vegetable dish that can be cooked in its serving dish. Because no water is added there is very little loss of nutrients; to maintain this, cook the vegetables at the last minute.

1. Using a food processor or grater, coarsely shred the vegetables.

2. Place them in a casserole, with the butter and sugar. Stir, cover and microwave on HIGH for 5 minutes.

3. Stir and season to taste. The vegetables should just be tender.

COURGETTES PROVENÇALE

SERVES 4

•

25 g (1 oz) butter

1 small onion, chopped

1 clove garlic, crushed

450 g (1 lb) courgettes, sliced

1 × 397 g (14 oz) can tomatoes

pinch of salt

15 ml (1 tbsp) chopped fresh parsley

salt and freshly ground black pepper

A good vegetable accompaniment to serve when courgettes are cheap or when you have a glut of them in the garden. Courgettes do not freeze very well on their own, but when prepared this way they freeze very successfully. Use skinned and chopped fresh tomatoes instead of canned when these are plentiful and cheap, or sprinkle with cheese to make a light meal. For a dinner party the dish can be completely cooked in advance and reheated at the last minute.

1. Microwave the butter in a casserole on HIGH for 1 minute. Stir in the onion and garlic, cover and microwave for 2 minutes on HIGH.

2. Stir in the courgettes, cover and microwave on HIGH for 5 minutes, stirring halfway through the cooking time.

3. Stir in the remaining ingredients, cover and microwave on HIGH for 5 minutes, stirring halfway through the cooking time. Serve.

POTATO SCALLOPS WITH RED ONIONS

SERVES 6

•

900 g (2 lb) floury old potatoes

50 g (2 oz) butter, plus 5 ml (1 tsp) to grease casserole

2 red onions, thinly sliced and separated into rings

300 ml (½ pt) vegetable or chicken stock

salt and freshly ground black pepper

 This attractive potato dish needs no last-minute attention other than a sprinkling of parsley for decoration. The finished result should give you crispy-topped potatoes in a rich onion sauce. Do take care when preparing the onions, wearing rubber gloves while slicing them: a hostess with purple hands is not an attractive sight, as we have found to our cost!

1. Peel the potatoes and cut into 5 mm (¼ in) slices.

2. Using 5 ml (1 tsp) of the butter, grease a 23 cm (9 in) casserole. Arrange the potato and onion slices alternately, standing them on their edges so that you see the top edge of the vegetable, not the cut face.

3. Pour over the stock and dot with the remaining butter. Bake in a preheated combination oven at 220°C with MEDIUM power microwave for 30 minutes or until tender and browned on top.

CASSEROLED NEW POTATOES WITH GARLIC

SERVES 6

•

1 kg (2¼ lb) new potatoes, scrubbed

50 g (2 oz) butter

4 cloves garlic (more if desired), peeled but left whole

30 ml (2 tbsp) water

bouquet garni or 10 ml (2 tsp) mixed dried herbs

salt and freshly ground black pepper

 This has become one of our favourite ways of cooking potatoes: it involves no mess and is very forgiving if kept waiting. Serve it in the casserole in which it is cooked, so that your guests can appreciate the wonderful aroma as you remove the lid. As new potatoes become larger during the season the cooking time will have to be increased. Prepare the potatoes several hours early if you want and cook up to an hour before eating, reheating in a hot oven if necessary.

1. Combine all the ingredients in an ovenproof casserole and cover well.

2. Bake in a preheated combination oven at 180°C with LOW power microwave for 25 minutes or until tender – the time will vary depending on the size of the potatoes.

3. Serve from the casserole straight at the table, spreading the garlic on the potatoes if desired.

SPICED POTATO STICKS

SERVES 4

•

675 g (1 ½ lb) potatoes

25 g (1 oz) butter

15 ml (1 tbsp) oil

5 ml (1 tsp) ground cumin

2.5 ml (½ tsp) ground coriander

2.5–5 ml (½-1 tsp) cayenne

salt and freshly ground black pepper

 These are like spicy chips and are delicious served with grilled meats or fish. If fresh coriander is available, use 1 tablespoon instead of the dried – this gives a delicious flavour and fresh appearance to the potatoes. The seasoning used in the dish may be varied, and a little finely chopped green pepper and onion can be added if desired. The potatoes can be prepared in advance and tossed in the melted butter and oil. Cook and serve them at the last minute, however, so that they are crisp.

1. Peel the potatoes and cut in 5 mm (¼ in) slices, then cut into matchsticks.

2. Place all the remaining ingredients in a shallow dish and microwave on HIGH for 1 minute.

3. Stir in the potatoes, then cook in a preheated combination oven at 220°C with LOW power microwave for 20–25 minutes or until crisp and golden stirring occasionally. Serve at once.

DUCHESSE POTATOES

SERVES 6–8 (MAKES 16)

•

900 g (2 lb) potatoes

60 ml (4 tbsp) water

25–50 g (1–2 oz) butter

1 egg beaten

milk (see method)

salt and freshly ground black pepper

These traditional piped and crisped potato cakes are good to serve at a dinner party, because apart from looking attractive they can be prepared in advance and just crisped at the last minute. A little nutmeg or grated Parmesan cheese can be added for a slightly different flavour.

1. Peel the potatoes and cut into large chunks.

2. Place the potatoes in a casserole with the water. Cover and microwave on HIGH for 12–15 minutes, rearranging occasionally.

3. Drain the potatoes, then mash with butter, egg and enough milk to give a soft, piping consistency. Season.

4. Spoon the potato into a piping bag with a large star nozzle, and pipe approximately 16 rounds on to a greased baking dish.

5. Bake in a preheated combination oven at 220°C, using conventional heat only for 20 minutes or until crisp and browned.

GAME CHIPS

SERVES 4–6
•
900 g (2 lb) potatoes

60–90 ml (4–6 tbsp) oil

These crispy potatoes are traditionally served with game, but can be tricky to prepare. Cooking in the combination oven takes the hard work out of the process and the result is lovely, crisp potato slices. Serve with any of the game recipes in the book. Game chips should not be cooked too far in advance as they will not stay crisp, but they do reheat fairly successfully in a hot oven.

1. Peel the potatoes and cut in 5 mm (¼ in) slices. Place in a bowl with the oil and toss to coat all the slices.

2. Spread the potato slices in a large shallow dish and cook in a preheated combination oven at 220°C with LOW power microwave for 20 minutes. Turn the potatoes over once during the cooking time.

—— COOK'S TIP——

The same method can be followed for roast potatoes, but cut these into chunks instead of slices. Allow a little extra cooking time.

SAVOURY BROWN RICE

SERVES 6
•
450 g (1 lb) long-grain brown rice

15 ml (1 tbsp) oil

1 small onion, finely chopped

1 litre (1¾ pt) boiling stock

salt

We find that brown rice cooks particularly well in the micro-wave, so long as the rice is soaked for 15 minutes in cold water before cooking. To give extra flavour, we have added a little onion to the rice and cooked it in stock. Chopped peppers or other vegetables could also be added. Use a stock of your choice, depending on what the rice is to be served with. We recently discovered some tomato stock cubes that are particularly good. The savoury rice needs to stand for 10 minutes before serving and will continue to absorb water, so do not be tempted to drain it when it comes out of the micro-wave. If you have a cup measure, the rule-of-thumb is 2 cups of brown rice to 4 cups of boiling stock, though if the rice is highly absorbent, you may need more liquid. The rice will stay hot in a covered dish for up to 30 minutes after coming out of the microwave.

1. Soak the rice in cold water to cover for 15 minutes, then drain.

2. Place the oil and onion in a casserole and microwave on HIGH for 2 minutes.

3. Stir in the rice, stock and salt to taste. Cover and microwave on HIGH for 20–25 minutes. Leave to stand, covered, for at least 10 minutes before serving.

COURGETTE TART

SERVES 6–8
•
Pastry

75 g (3 oz) butter
175 g (6 oz) plain flour
30 ml (2 tbsp) Parmesan cheese
45 ml (3 tbsp) cold water

Filling

25 g (1 oz) butter
2 shallots, finely chopped
350 g (12 oz) courgettes, cut into 1 cm (½ in) cubes
1 sprig of fresh rosemary or 2.5 ml (½ tsp) dried rosemary
150 ml (5 fl oz) single cream
2 large eggs, beaten
45 ml (3 tbsp) grated Parmesan cheese
salt and freshly ground black pepper

This is a dish that became popular after a business partner returned from Italy with several kilos of Parmesan. The tart has a delicate flavour and makes a good starter or lunch dish. Try to use the freshly grated Parmesan – the ready-grated type in a tub has nowhere near as good a flavour. If you want to make this in advance, roll out the pastry and line but do not fill the flan dish; slice the courgettes but do not cook them.

1. Rub the butter into the flour until it resembles fine breadcrumbs, add the Parmesan and stir in enough of the water to bind.

2. Roll out the pastry to line a 20 cm (8 in) flan dish or ring suitable for your oven. Leave to rest.

3. Make the filling: put the butter and shallots into a dish and microwave on HIGH for 3 minutes.

4. Add the courgettes and rosemary and microwave on HIGH for 6 minutes stirring once.

5. Remove the rosemary if possible and cool the courgettes. (If you have used dried rosemary you will not be able to remove it.)

6. Stir in the cream, eggs and Parmesan. Season to taste. Pour into the prepared flan case and cook in a preheated combination oven at 200°C with LOW power microwave for 20 minutes. It should barely colour. Serve warm.

PISTACHIO PAELLA

SERVES 4
•

450 g (1 lb) long-grain brown rice

30 ml (2 tbsp) oil

1 onion, chopped

1 clove garlic, crushed

1 fresh green chilli, seeded and sliced

5 sticks celery, sliced

1 red pepper, seeded and sliced

125 g (4 oz) pistachio nuts

5 ml (1 tsp) dried basil

1.2 litres (2 pt) hot tomato stock

salt and freshly ground black pepper

black olives to garnish

This paella is good to serve hot as a main course or cold as part of a salad. If tomato stock cubes are not available, substitute 1 × 397 g (14 oz) can chopped tomatoes, puréed and made up to 1.2 litres (2 pt) with boiling water. The addition of tomatoes gives a lovely rich colour to the paella. A few of the chilli seeds can be added if you like it hot. The paella reheats quite successfully although you may need to add a little extra water. You may use a cup measure for the rice and stock, in which case you will need 2 cups brown rice to 5 cups stock.

1. Soak the rice in cold water to cover for 15 minutes, then rinse and drain.

2. Place the oil in a casserole and stir in the onion, garlic, chilli, celery and red pepper. Cover and microwave on HIGH for 5 minutes, stirring halfway through the cooking time.

3. Stir in the rice, pistachio nuts, basil and stock. Season well. Microwave uncovered, on HIGH for 25 minutes.

4. Cover and leave to stand for 10 minutes, then garnish with black olives and serve.

CELERIAC BASKET WITH VEGETABLE MEDLEY

SERVES 4
•

225 g (8 oz) celeriac

225 g (8 oz) potatoes

30 ml (2 tbsp) water

40 g (1½ oz) butter

1 egg

salt and freshly ground black pepper

1 small onion, sliced

225 g (8 oz) courgettes, sliced

125 g (4 oz) button mushrooms, sliced

225 g (8 oz) tomatoes, skinned and chopped

50 g (2 oz) Cheddar cheese, grated

Celeriac is an ugly looking vegetable, but its looks are certainly not reflected in its flavour. It does have a tendency to discolour very quickly, so cook it without delay or, if it is to be used in a salad, dip in lemon juice and water. To serve celeriac as a vegetable, boil equal quantities of it with potatoes and mash with butter and seasoning. The following recipe makes an attractive accompaniment or, with a little extra cheese, a vegetarian dish. Try filling the basket with flageolet beans cooked in garlic and tomato sauce for a more substantial meal.

1.   Peel the celeriac and potatoes and cut both vegetables into roughly 2.5 cm (1 in) cubes. Place in a casserole with the water. Cover and microwave on HIGH for 12–15 minutes or until tender.

2.   Drain the vegetables and mash with 15 g (½ oz) of the butter. Beat in the egg and season to taste.

3.   Use the pureé to line a buttered 20 cm (8 in) flan dish, moulding up the sides with the back of a wooden spoon.

4.   Cook in a preheated combination oven at 220°C for 10 minutes or until lightly browned. If your oven has a grill, this may be used instead.

5.   Microwave the remaining butter in a casserole on HIGH for 1 minute until melted. Add the onion and microwave on HIGH for 2 minutes. Stir in the courgettes and mushrooms, cover and microwave on HIGH for 4 minutes, stirring halfway through the cooking time.

6.   Stir the tomatoes into the vegetable mixture, then pour into the celeriac basket. Sprinkle over the cheese and cook in a preheated combination oven at 220°C with LOW power microwave for 5 minutes or until the cheese has melted. Serve at once.

LASAGNE RING MOULD

SERVES 4–6
•

250 g (8 oz) green lasagne

salt and freshly ground black pepper

5 ml (1 tsp) oil

25 g (1 oz) butter

1 large onion, finely chopped

125 g (4 oz) button mushrooms, wiped and chopped

125 g (4 oz) Cheddar cheese, grated

2 eggs

300 ml (½ pt) double cream

150 ml (5 fl oz) milk

Serve this attractive pasta dish as a main course or slice it as a starter. This dish would normally be cooked in a bain marie, but by using the combination oven this is unnecessary. The centre of the pasta ring may be filled with fresh vegetable or watercress. This dish reheats successfully.

1. Cook the lasagne on the conventional hob in a large saucepan of boiling salted water with the oil added.

2. Use the pasta to line a buttered 900 ml (1½ pt) pyrex ring mould, over-lapping the pieces.

3. Microwave the remaining butter in a bowl on HIGH for 1 minute until melted. Add the onion and microwave on HIGH for 2 minutes, then add the mushrooms and cook for 2 minutes more.

4. Combine the cheese, eggs, cream and milk in a bowl. Mix well, then stir into the vegetable mixture. Season to taste.

5. Pour the mixture into the lasagne-lined mould and fold over any overlapping pasta. Cover with buttered greaseproof paper and cook in a preheated combination oven at 180°C with LOW power microwave for 20 minutes. Stand for a few minutes before removing the paper and turning out.

LENTIL MOUSSAKA

SERVES 4

•

2 aubergines

salt and freshly ground black pepper

175 g (6 oz) red lentils

600 ml (1 pt) water

90 ml (6 tbsp) oil

1 large onion, sliced

1 clove garlic, crushed

125 g (4 oz) button mushrooms, wiped and sliced

1 × 397 g (14 oz) can tomatoes

5 ml (1 tsp) cayenne

Topping

300 ml (½ pt) milk

2 eggs

15 ml (1 tbsp) plain flour

50 g (2 oz) grated Parmesan cheese

 This is a tasty and colourful vegetarian dish. Although making it involves several stages, once made it will sit quite happily and can be reheated to serve. It is equally good served cold with a salad.

1. Slice the aubergines on to a plate, sprinkle with salt and set aside for 30 minutes.

2. Meanwhile pick over the lentils, then rinse and place in a deep casserole with the water. Microwave on HIGH for 15 minutes or until the lentils are soft and most of the liquid has been absorbed.

3. Rinse the aubergines thoroughly and pat dry with paper towels. Heat 60 ml (4 tbsp) of the oil in a large frying pan on a conventional hob and quickly fry the aubergine slices on both sides.

4. Place the remaining oil in a casserole and stir in the onion and garlic. Microwave on HIGH for 3 minutes. Stir in the mushrooms and microwave on HIGH for a further 2 minutes.

5. Stir in the lentils, tomatoes, cayenne and salt and pepper to taste.

6. Place a layer of aubergine slices in the base of a casserole. Add a layer of lentil mixture. Repeat until all the layers are used up, ending with aubergines.

7. To make the topping, place the milk, eggs and flour in a blender or food processor and blend until smooth. Pour the mixture into a bowl and microwave on HIGH for 3–4 minutes, stirring occasionally until slightly thickened. (This can be done in a saucepan on a conventional hob if the microwave is in use.) Season to taste.

8. Pour the topping over the aubergines, sprinkle with grated Parmesan and cook in a preheated combination oven at 200°C with LOW power microwave for 20 minutes. Serve at once.

DESSERTS

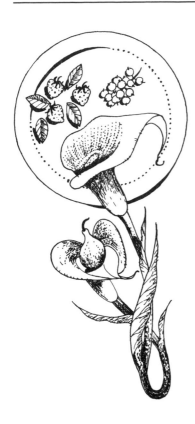

*T*HE CROWNING GLORY of a meal is often the dessert. It provides the last flavour that lingers in the mouth the longest. When entertaining more than 4 guests it is a good idea to offer a choice of desserts, balancing richness, texture and flavour. Some people will always go for the rich dessert; others prefer something lighter and less sweet. The advantage of two or more desserts is that there is sometimes some left for the next day, although from past experience, many of our guests want to try everything and find it so delicious that it all gets polished off.

The combination oven enables the cook to produce a wide range of desserts, from crisp pastry to light mousses. The microwave is especially useful for melting chocolate and softening gelatine, while the oven gives golden flans and light sponges.

GATEAU BANANE

SERVES 6–8
•
50 g (2 oz) butter

150 g (5 oz) soft dark brown sugar

1 egg

1 ripe banana, peeled and cut into
chunks

2.5 ml (½ tsp) vanilla essence

45 ml (3 tbsp) dark rum

150 g (5 oz) self-raising flour

2.5 ml (½ tsp) bicarbonate of soda

To Decorate

300 ml (½ pt) double cream

1 ripe banana

15 ml (1 tbsp) caster sugar

50 g (2 oz) plain chocolate

This is must for banana lovers – a really fresh-tasting gateau, which is very light and moist. The dark sugar gives an excellent colour which contrasts well with the cream topping. The cake itself freezes successfully but do not decorate too early or the cream will darken.

1. Soften the butter if necessary by microwaving on LOW for 1 minute.

2. Combine the butter, sugar, egg, banana, vanilla essence and rum in a blender or food processor and blend until smooth. Pour into a bowl. Sift together the flour and bicarbonate of soda and fold into the mixture.

3. Pour into a greased and base-lined 20 cm (8 in) cake dish and bake in a pre-heated combination oven at 190°C with LOW power microwave for about 12 minutes, or until a skewer inserted in the centre comes out clean.

4. Leave the cake to stand in the dish for a few minutes before turning out on to a wire rack to cool.

5. In a bowl whip the cream until thick. Mash the banana and beat into the cream with the sugar.

6. Split the cake in half and fill the centre with half the cream. Replace the lid and top with the remaining cream.

7. Microwave the chocolate on HIGH for 1 minute to melt. Drizzle it over the cake, or pipe in a zig-zag pattern.

CHOCOLATE ROULADE

SERVES 6
•
oil to grease tin

125 g (4 oz) plain chocolate

3 eggs, separated

125 g (4 oz) caster sugar

30 ml (2 tbsp) hot water

300 ml (½ pt) whipping cream

sifted icing sugar to decorate

We have included this recipe, even though it is well known, because it is so delicious and also because many people do not realise that it is so simple to make. As the roulade needs to be left in the tin for 3 hours before rolling up, it must be made well ahead of a dinner party. Do not try to rush it or the result will be disastrous! Once filled with cream, the roulade will sit quite happily in the refrigerator for several hours before serving.

1. Line a 35 × 25 cm (14 × 10 in) Swiss roll tin with greaseproof paper, then generously brush the paper with oil (see Cook's tip).

2. Break up the chocolate, place in a bowl and microwave on HIGH for about 2 minutes. Stir until melted, then stir in the hot water. Preheat the combination oven, using only conventional heat, to 180°C.

3. Whisk the egg yolks and caster sugar together in a mixing bowl until they are light in colour and texture. Stir in the chocolate mixture.

4. Beat the egg whites until stiff, and fold carefully into the chocolate mixture. Pour into the tin and spread lightly to the corners. Bake for 15–20 minutes or until a skewer inserted in the cake comes out clean. Leaving the cake in the tin, cover with greaseproof paper and a damp tea towel. Set aside for 3 hours.

5. Whip the cream until stiff. Dust a sheet of greaseproof paper with icing sugar, then invert the roulade on to it. Peel off the lining paper, spread with cream and roll up like a Swiss roll.

6. Dust with more icing sugar, place on a serving dish, then chill for 1 hour before serving.

—— COOK'S TIP——

A Swiss roll tin will not fit in some ovens with fixed turntables. Use a square tin instead.

LEMON AND PRIMROSE GATEAU

SERVES 8
•
4 eggs (size 1)

125 g (4 oz) caster sugar

125 g (4 oz) self-raising flour

chocolate rose leaves and frosted primroses to decorate

Filling

150 ml (5 fl oz) double cream

150 ml (5 fl oz) Greek strained yogurt

225 g (8 oz) Lemon curd (see page 130)

This is the most amazing cake, guaranteed to bring gasps of delight from your guests. To frost the primroses you simply brush the flowers carefully with beaten egg white and then sprinkle them with caster sugar, before leaving them to dry overnight in a warm place like an airing cupboard. To make the chocolate rose leaves, see the Cook's tip on page 138. Make the cake in advance and freeze if necessary. Fill an hour or so before serving. If carefully stored the chocolate leaves will keep well for some time as will the frosted primroses.

1. Put the eggs and sugar into the warmed bowl of a mixer and beat until light and foamy and leaving a trail.

2. Sift the flour and cut into the egg mixture with a wire whisk.

3. Pour the mixture into a greased base-lined and sugared 23 cm (9 in) cake dish or tin suitable for your oven.

4. Bake in a preheated combination oven at 200°C with LOW power microwave for 12 minutes or until the surface of the cake springs back when pressed.

5. Invert on to a wire rack to cool.

6. Whip the cream. Combine half with the yogurt and lemon curd, taking care not to overmix, or the mixture will become too runny. Split the cake in half with a sharp knife and sandwich together with the lemon mixture. Pipe the remaining cream on the top and decorate with the chocolate leaves and frosted primroses.

PEAR AND CARAMEL BAVAROIS

SERVES 6–8
•
250 g (9 oz) granulated sugar

120 ml (4 fl oz) water

300 ml (½ pt) milk

20 ml (4 tsp) gelatine

3 eggs

250 ml (8 fl oz) sweet cider or white wine

900 g (2 lb) pears, quartered, peeled and cored

150 ml (5 fl oz) double cream, whipped

cigarettes Russes to serve

This has to be one of our favourite desserts. The pale coffee-coloured stripes make the dessert attractive to the eye, but the flavour is even better! A friend saw a traditional French bavarois recipe while browsing through an old magazine at the doctor's, but felt the use of almost a dozen eggs was a little excessive! This is our version, using only three eggs. We hope you will enjoy it. The dessert may successfully be prepared the day before serving.

1. Place 175 g (6 oz) of the sugar in a bowl. Add 90 ml (6 tbsp) of the water and microwave on HIGH for 5 minutes. Stir until the sugar has dissolved, then return to the oven and microwave on HIGH for 5–6 minutes or until a good caramel is achieved.

2. Meanwhile, on a conventional hob, bring the milk to just below boiling point in a saucepan. Set aside. Sprinkle 10 ml (2 tsp) of the gelatine over 15 ml (1 tbsp) of the remaining water and set aside.

3. When the caramel is ready, remove it from the oven and very carefully pour a little of the scalded milk over it. It will splutter and bubble fiercely. Pour over the remaining milk and stir until the caramel is dissolved.

4. Dissolve the softened gelatine in the microwave on HIGH for 15 seconds. Whisk the eggs into the caramel-flavoured milk and microwave on HIGH for 3 minutes, whisking thoroughly every minute. Whisk in the dissolved gelatine, then stand the bowl in cold water to cool the caramel custard.

5. Combine the cider and remaining 75 g (3 oz) sugar in a casserole and microwave on HIGH for 4 minutes. Stir to dissolve the sugar, then add the pears. Cover and microwave on HIGH for 15 minutes.

6. Meanwhile sprinkle the remaining 10 ml (2 tsp) gelatine over the remaining 15 ml (1 tbsp) water. Allow to stand for a few minutes, then microwave on HIGH for 15 seconds until dissolved.

7. With a slotted spoon, carefully transfer two-thirds of the cooked pears to a

blender or food processor. Purée until smooth, then beat in the dissolved gelatine. Set aside.

8. Transfer the remaining pears with all the cooking juices to the blender or food processor and process to a smooth sauce. Transfer to a serving jug and refrigerate until required.

9. Fold the whipped cream into the caramel custard, then pour half the mixture into a greased 900 g (2 lb) loaf tin. Chill quickly in the freezer until set. Pour over the pear and gelatine mixture. Chill again until set, then pour over the remaining caramel custard.

10. Chill the bavarois in the refrigerator until set, then dip the tin quickly in hot water and turn out on to a serving platter. Serve in slices, accompanied by the pear purée and cigarettes Russes.

CHOCOLATE WALNUT PIE

SERVES 8
•
Pastry

125 g (4 oz) butter

225 g (8 oz) plain flour

60 ml (4 tbsp) water

Filling

50 g (2 oz) cocoa

2 eggs

225 g (8 oz) light soft brown sugar

1 × 170 g (6 oz) can evaporated milk

5 ml (1 tsp) vanilla essence

50 g (2 oz) butter, melted

175 g (6 oz) walnuts, roughly chopped

This is incredibly rich so small slices are in order. It is based on an American recipe, but we have cut down the sugar considerably. Traditionally it would have been made with pecans but walnuts are a good alternative. Try adding the grated rind of an orange to the filling for a change. This can be made the day before it is required if you wish.

1. Rub the fat into the flour until it resembles fine breadcrumbs. Stir in enough of the cold water to form a dough.

2. Roll out the pastry and use to line a 25 cm (10 in) flan dish. Leave to rest in a refrigerator while you make the filling.

3. Mix together all the filling ingredients except the walnuts. Beat well, then fold in the walnuts.

4. Pour the filling into the prepared flan case and bake in a preheated combination oven at 190°C with LOW power microwave for 20–25 minutes.

5. Serve with plenty of lightly whipped cream.

TUILES

MAKES 24

•

50 g (2 oz) butter

50 g (2 oz) icing sugar, sifted

1 egg white (size 3)

50 g (2 oz) plain flour, sifted

 Tuiles means "tiles", which is what these biscuits look like. Some of the recipes for this never seem to work but we seem to have no trouble with this one. The only difficulty might be with the first tray, which is why heating it is suggested. The tuiles may be made in advance and stored in an airtight container.

1. Preheat the combination oven, using only conventional heat, to 220°C.

2. In a mixing bowl, cream the butter and sugar together until very soft (microwave for a few seconds on HIGH if the butter is too hard).

3. Whisk the egg white to soft peaks and fold it into the butter mixture with the flour.

4. Grease and flour a baking sheet, and warm it slightly in the preheated oven.

5. Spread 3 or 4 circles of the mixture on to the baking sheet. Cook in the preheated oven for 5–6 minutes or until the edges are lightly browned.

6. Remove from the oven and leave for no longer than 1 minute before removing from the baking sheet. Cool over a rolling pin.

7. Repeat with the rest of the mixture.

—— COOK'S TIP——

A tuile basket makes a pretty container for sorbet or mousse. Make the biscuits fairly large (2 to a baking sheet), and shape them over an inverted jar or bowl.

CAMEMBERT PASTRIES WITH GOOSEBERRY PURÉE

SERVES 6
•
450 g (1 lb) puff pastry

25 g (1 oz) butter

1 egg, lightly beaten

175 g (6 oz) Camembert cheese

1 × 284 g (10 oz) can gooseberries, drained

15 ml (1 tbsp) golden syrup, optional

mint leaves to decorate

This is a delicious savoury/sweet idea to serve at the end of the meal, ideal for those guests who do not go for rich, sugary desserts. We enrich the puff pastry by adding extra butter (see step 1 below). This gives a wonderfully light result. When available fresh gooseberries can be used for the purée, in which case add sugar or syrup to taste.

The pastries are ideally frozen prior to cooking. They can then be cooked from frozen at the last minute. The sauce can also be frozen and reheated in the microwave.

1. Roll out the pastry to an oblong approximately 25 × 15 cm (10 × 6 in). Dot one half with butter then fold over, seal the edges and roll out to a square approximately 40 × 30 cm (16 × 12 in).

2. Cut into 12 squares, each 10 × 10 cm (4 × 4 in). Brush the edges of each square with beaten egg then divide the Camembert between them.

3. Wrap each pastry up like a small parcel, tucking the edges underneath. Place on a baking sheet. Chill in the freezer for 10 minutes. Preheat the combination oven, using only conventional heat, to 225°C.

4. Brush the Camembert pastries with egg and bake in the preheated oven for 12 minutes or until golden brown.

5. To make the fruit purée, place the gooseberries in a blender or food processor with the golden syrup, if used. Blend until smooth. Pour into a jug and microwave on HIGH for 2 minutes until hot.

6. Coat individual plates with purée and serve 2 parcels on tops of each, decorated with fresh mint leaves.

APPLE IN THE CLOUDS

SERVES 4

•

Filling

350 g (12 oz) cooking apples

15 ml (1 tbsp) water

50 g (2 oz) sugar

50 g (2 oz) butter

1 egg

50 g (2 oz) raisins

Pastry

450 g (1 lb) puff pastry

50 g (2 oz) butter

beaten egg to glaze

The pastry in this is so light that the children say it is like eating clouds – hence the name! The tip of rolling extra butter into frozen puff pastry is well worth copying in other recipes. The day before a dinner party is the time to make the apple filling, then in the morning make the pie, decorate and keep chilled or even freeze until you are ready to cook and serve it. With your combination oven it can even cook while you eat the main course! Do make sure your oven is really hot; otherwise the result will not be as good. Allow a few extra minutes if you are cooking it from frozen.

1. Peel, core and slice the apples into a casserole. Add the water, cover and microwave on HIGH for 8 minutes.

2. Stir well and add the sugar and the butter. Microwave on HIGH, stirring occasionally, for a further 6 minutes or until thick.

3. Beat the egg and stir in a spoonful of the apple mixture. Mix well and repeat. This should help to prevent the mixture curdling.

4. Add the egg to the apple and beat well. Microwave on HIGH for 2 minutes, stir in the raisins, cover and leave to get cold and set before continuing.

5. Cut the pastry in half and roll each half out until it is about 15 cm (6 in) square.

6. Spread one half of the pastry with the softened butter (microwaved on MEDIUM for 30 seconds if it is too hard) then cover with the other piece. With a rolling pin press along each edge to seal. Now roll the pastry out until it is just big enough to allow you to cut out two 20 cm (8 in) circles.

7. Brush with water 4 cm (1½ in) round the edge of one of the circles, then pile the cold apple filling in the centre. Roll the second pastry circle a little larger and use it to cover the first. Seal carefully, making sure there is no air trapped inside. Scallop the edges and put the pie on a baking sheet. Brush it with egg and chill for at least 30 minutes.

8. Pierce the crust in the centre and make a spiral design with a sharp knife. Take care not to cut through the crust.

9. Bake in a preheated combination oven at 220°C with LOW power microwave for 12–14 minutes or until golden. Serve immediately with lots of single cream, if liked.

HAZELNUT AND STRAWBERRY GALETTE

SERVES 8

•

50 g (2 oz) hazelnuts

125 g (4 oz) plain flour

75 g (3 oz) butter

50 g (2 oz) caster sugar

Soufflé

225 g (8 oz) fresh strawberries, hulled

3 eggs, separated

75 g (3 oz) caster sugar

15 g (½ oz) gelatine

juice of 1 large lemon

150 ml (5 fl oz) double cream

To Decorate

whipped cream

8 strawberries

A light strawberry soufflé this, sandwiched between layers of crisp hazelnut pastry. It looks very attractive and is delicious to eat. The hazelnuts are best skinned, and this can easily be done with the aid of the microwave. The hazelnut biscuits can be made well in advance and the galette assembled in the late afternoon to eat in the evening. Do not leave it too long or the pastry will lose its crispness.

1. Skin the hazelnuts: put them on a plate and microwave on HIGH for 5–7 minutes. When cool enough to handle, rub off the skins, then grind the nuts to fine crumbs.

2. Place the flour in a bowl and rub in the butter until the mixture resembles breadcrumbs. Stir in the sugar and ground hazelnuts. Knead together lightly to form a firm dough, then chill in the refrigerator for 30 minutes.

3. Roll out the pastry to two 20 cm (8 in) rounds. Place one round in the base of a greased and base-lined 20 cm (8 in) loose-bottomed cake tin. Place the other round on greaseproof paper on a baking dish.

4. Preheat the combination oven, using only conventional heat, to 180°C. Bake the pastry rounds for 12 minutes. In some ovens they will need to be cooked one at a time. Remove from the oven, and leave the base in the cake tin to cool. When cooled a little, cut the second round into 8 wedges to go on top of the soufflé.

5. To make the soufflé, purée the strawberries in a blender or food processor until smooth. Pour the purée into a bowl and add the egg yolks and sugar. Whisk until the mixture thickens and becomes lighter in colour.

6. Sprinkle the gelatine over the lemon juice, stand for a few minutes, then dissolve in the microwave on HIGH for 30 seconds. Whisk into the strawberry mixture.

7. Whip the cream until it will almost hold its shape, then fold into the mixture. Refrigerate until just beginning to set, then whisk the egg whites until light and fluffy and fold into the mixture.

8. Pour the mixture on top of the base in the cake tin, then arrange the cut wedges on top. Chill in the refrigerator until set.

9. To serve, carefully remove the galette from the tin. Slide it on to a serving plate and decorate each wedge with a swirl of whipped cream and a fresh strawberry.

GINGER LEMON FLAN

SERVES 6–8

•

175 g (6 oz) plain flour

2.5 ml (½ tsp) bicarbonate of soda

5 ml (1 tsp) ground ginger

50 g (2 oz) butter, softened

75 g (3 oz) soft brown sugar

30 ml (2 tbsp) golden syrup

1 egg, separated

icing sugar to decorate

Filling

2 eggs

75 g (3 oz) caster sugar

grated rind and juice of
2 lemons

150 ml (¼ pt) double cream

 Lemon and ginger go together really well. Resist eating this flan until the day after baking to allow the flavours to develop. The base will taste like a soft ginger biscuit by the time you eat it, and the filling is a very lemony custard. Do not worry if the top cracks slightly as this does not affect the wonderful taste.

1. Sift the flour, bicarbonate of soda and ginger together. Rub in the butter and stir in the sugar.

2. Microwave the syrup on HIGH power for 30 seconds so that it is easy to pour. Add it with the egg yolk to the flour. Mix well.

3. Knead the pastry together adding a little of the egg white if necessary. Roll out to line a 20 cm (8 in) flan dish, pricking the base well.

4. Bake the base blind in a preheated combination oven at 200°C with LOW power microwave for 5 minutes. Remove it from the oven and gently push it back into shape.

5. Mix all the filling ingredients together and whisk lightly. Pour into the prepared base.

6. Bake in a preheated combination oven set this time to 180°C with LOW power microwave for 15–18 minutes. It should not be brown, but the custard should be set.

7. When cool, leave for 24 hours. Dust with icing sugar before serving.

GRAPE AND ALMOND TART

SERVES 6–8

•

75 g (3 oz) butter

75 g (3 oz) caster sugar

3 egg yolks

175 g (6 oz) plain flour

25 g (1 oz) flaked almonds

Filling

350 g (12 oz) white grapes, deseeded – muscat grapes are best

2 eggs

50 g (2 oz) ground almonds

50 g (2 oz) caster sugar

150 ml (5 fl oz) single cream

25 g (1 oz) flaked almonds

125 g (4 oz) apricot jam

15 ml (1 tbsp) water

 In the autumn, when muscat grapes are in season, this is a lovely dessert to make. It is a little tedious, removing all the pips but worth the trouble. It is best to make the flan the day you want to serve it, although any left over will be almost as good the next day. Do not prepare the grapes too far in advance of cooking because they will become very wet and spoil the tart.

1.   Cream the butter, sugar and egg yolks together until soft.

2.   Stir in the flour and almonds and mix together until a dough is formed. Chill for 30 minutes.

3.   Roll out the pastry to line a 20 cm (8 in) flan dish. Preheat a combination oven, using only conventional heat, to 200°C.

4.   Bake the pastry case blind (see Cook's tip) for 10 minutes. Remove from the oven.

5.   For the filling, place the grapes in the flan case. Mix together the eggs, ground almonds, caster sugar and cream; pour over the grapes. Sprinkle the flaked almonds over the top.

6.   Reset the preheated combination oven to 180°C with LOW power microwave and bake the tart for 20 minutes. It should be pale gold and set. Cool the flan.

7.   Microwave the jam on HIGH for 2 minutes to melt. Stir in the water and sieve the jam; reheat if necessary.

8.   Brush the melted jam over the tart, starting from the centre and working towards the rim until all the top is covered.

—— COOK'S TIP ——

To bake blind, line the flan case with greaseproof paper and fill with baking beans. Bake as directed above, then remove the paper and beans.

MOCHA GATEAU

SERVES 8
•
125 g (4 oz) ground almonds

125 g (4 oz) caster sugar

3 large eggs plus 2 egg whites

25 g (1 oz) plain flour

25 g (1 oz) butter, melted

Filling

175 g (6 oz) plain chocolate

30 ml (2 tbsp) milk

5 ml (1 tsp) instant coffee

3 egg yolks plus 1 egg white

10 ml (2 tsp) gelatine

30 ml (2 tbsp) water

150 ml (5 fl oz) double cream

This is an ideal dinner party dessert because it can be made a couple of days in advance and kept covered in the refrigerator. The light moist almond sponge is sandwiched together with a rich mocha mousse to make a delicious finale, definitely not for those on a diet! It looks especially pretty served in slices on individual plates: pour a pool of double cream on to each plate, drop in a tiny amount of coffee syrup (see Cook's tip) and pull a knife through to give a feathered effect. Set a slice of the gateau on each prepared plate to serve.

1. Preheat the combination oven, using only conventional heat, to 200°C.

2. Combine the almonds and caster sugar in a mixer or food processor. Add 1 of the eggs and beat well, then add the remaining whole eggs, beating well after each addition.

3. Beat the egg whites until stiff. Using a wire whisk, fold them into the almond mixture with the sifted flour and melted butter.

4. Pour the mixture into a greased and base-lined 23 cm (9 in) cake tin and bake for 15–20 minutes. The cake should be firm to the touch and golden brown in colour.

5. Cool the cake in the tin for 5 minutes, then turn out on to a wire rack. When completely cool, trim the cake to fit a 20 cm (8 in) loose-bottomed cake tin. Split the cake in half through the middle. You should have 2 thin circles of cake that exactly fit the loose-bottomed tin.

6. For the filling, break the chocolate into pieces and put in a bowl. Microwave on HIGH until melted. This will take from 4–8 minutes depending on the thickness of the chocolate. Mix the milk and coffee together and add to the melted chocolate. Stir thoroughly, then add the egg yolks. Mix well.

7. Sprinkle the gelatine on to the water in a cup. Leave to stand for 1 minute, then microwave on HIGH for 30–60 seconds to dissolve.

8. In a large mixing bowl, beat the egg white until stiff. In a second bowl, beat the cream to soft peaks. Using a wire whisk, fold the cream, chocolate mixture and gelatine into the egg white and mix gently.

9. Base-line the loose-bottomed cake tin and put one of the sponge rounds in the base. Cover with the chocolate mixture and top with the remaining sponge round. Leave to set in a cool place.

10. Run a hot knife between the cake and the tin to unmould before transferring the gateau to a serving plate. You can use a hot knife to repair the side of the mousse if necessary.

—— COOK'S TIP——
To make the coffee syrup, combine 5 ml (1 tsp) water,
2.5 ml (½ tsp) instant coffee and 5 ml (1 tsp) caster sugar in a cup.
Microwave on HIGH for 30 seconds to melt the sugar. Stir and use as
suggested above.

ORANGES WITH CARAMEL CREAM

SERVES 6

•

125 g (4 oz) caster sugar

30 ml (2 tbsp) water

300 ml (½ pt) whipping or double cream

2 egg yolks

30 ml (2 tbsp) brandy

6 large oranges

This is a simple yet sophisticated sweet; those on a diet can just eat the oranges and miss out on the sauce, although it really is too good to miss. The contrast of the hot oranges and the cold sauce is unusual. We like it, but if you don't, serve the oranges cold. Make the sauce well in advance so it has time to chill. The prepared oranges may be arranged on the serving plates and covered. Alternatively, reassemble the sliced oranges, secure each with a cocktail stick and store covered in a bowl so they don't dry up.

1. Put the sugar into a large bowl (not plastic), stir in the water and microwave uncovered on HIGH for 1 minute.

2. Stir until all the sugar is dissolved. Then microwave on HIGH without stirring for 4–5 minutes or until the caramel is golden brown.

3. Remove the bowl from the oven and carefully add half the cream. It will spit, so stand well back. Beat in the egg yolks and brandy and the rest of the cream, microwave on HIGH for 1 minute, stir well and pour into a serving jug to cool. Do not worry if there are still lumps of caramel; these will dissolve. Chill in the refrigerator until required.

4. With a potato peeler, cut a few strips of rind from the oranges. Remove the pith and cut the strips into fine julienne. Reserve.

5. With a sharp knife cut a slice from the top and bottom of each orange, then standing each fruit on a cut edge, remove the peel in sections by cutting from top to bottom.

6. Slice an orange in thin rounds, arrange on a plate and scatter a few julienne strips over the top. Repeat with the remaining oranges.

7. Just before serving microwave the oranges (2 plates at a time) on HIGH until hot. Each pair of plates will require 1½ minutes. Stir the chilled sauce and serve separately.

BRANDY SNAP HORNS WITH RASPBERRY SAUCE

SERVES 6
•
Sauce

225 g (½ lb) fresh or frozen raspberries

30 ml (2 tbsp) water

icing sugar to taste

Snaps

125 g (4 oz) butter

125 g (4 oz) caster sugar

60 ml (4 tbsp) golden syrup

125 g (4 oz) plain flour

5 ml (1 tsp) ground ginger

12 × 15 cm (6 in) square pieces of non-stick silicone paper

To Serve

300 ml (½ pt) whipping cream

some fresh raspberry leaves or mint leaves

 This is the most beautiful-looking sweet: dark raspberry sauce framing crisp biscuits filled with cream, decorated with whole raspberries and leaves. It is easy too. In fact, when in a real hurry we have been known to buy ready-made brandy snaps. Try this method of serving with cream-filled meringues; they look equally stunning. If you don't have cream horn moulds, use a greased wooden spoon handle. You can even drape the biscuits over a small orange. If the biscuits become difficult to roll, pop back into the oven for a few minutes to soften them, although our method using individual squares of non-stick silicone paper helps considerably. Make the brandy snaps up to 1 week in advance and store in an airtight box. Fill just before serving. The sauce can be made in advance and frozen. If you are going to use it a lot make it in bulk.

1. First make the sauce. Reserve 12 raspberries. Place the rest in a bowl and microwave on HIGH for 4 minutes if fresh, or 10 minutes on LOW plus 4 minutes on HIGH if frozen. The juice should just have started to run.

2. Purée the raspberries with the water in a blender or food processor, then sieve to remove the pips which would spoil the flavour and appearance.

3. Sweeten to taste with the icing sugar and chill.

4. For the snaps, microwave the butter, sugar and syrup together on HIGH for 2 minutes until melted. Stir in the flour and ginger. Preheat the combination oven, using only conventional heat to 180°C.

5. Drop teaspoons of the mixture on to the squares of paper on a baking sheet, allowing plenty of space for spreading – only do 4 at a time. Bake for 7–9 minutes.

6. Allow the biscuits to cool for 1–2 minutes, then loosen with a palette knife and peel off the paper. Wrap, smooth side in, around a greased cream horn mould.

7. Repeat with the rest of the mixture, warming the cooked biscuits if they become too cold to shape successfully.

8. When the horns are cold fill them with whipped cream. Flood 6 large individual serving plates with the raspberry sauce, place 2 or 3 filled horns on each and garnish with the reserved berries and some fresh raspberry or mint leaves.

RASPBERRY-FILLED ALMOND TARTS

SERVES 6
•
125 g (4 oz) unsalted butter

125 g (4 oz) ground almonds

125 g (4 oz) caster sugar

Filling

150 ml (5 fl oz) double cream

175 g (6 oz) fresh raspberries

a few raspberry leaves to garnish

 This recipe makes macaroon-like tarts, absolutely delicious and very easy. Try filling them with a mixture of black and red currants for a change or even mince meat at Christmas. The tarts can be made a few days in advance and stored in an airtight container if required. Fill just before serving.

1. Soften the butter and mix in the almonds and sugar, using a mixer or food processor if desired. Preheat the combination oven, using only conventional heat, to 190°C.

2. Put teaspoons of the mixture into bun tins. (There is no need to grease these.) You will make about 20. Do not spread the mixture.

3. Bake in the preheated oven for 10–15 minutes – watching the tarts carefully towards the end because they will easily burn. They should be golden brown.

4. Remove from the oven and cool for a couple of minutes. Loosen from the tin but do not remove until almost cold.

5. Just before serving fill the tarts with the lightly whipped cream and the raspberries. Decorate with the leaves.

CHOUX BUNS WITH COFFEE CREAM AND CARAMEL

SERVES 6
•
Choux Buns

150 ml (5 fl oz) water

50 g (2 oz) butter

65 g (2½ oz) plain flour

2 eggs, (size 3), lightly beaten

Confectioners' Custard

150 ml (5 fl oz) milk

10 ml (2 tsp) cornflour

1 egg, lightly beaten

25 g (1 oz) sugar

150 ml (5 fl oz) double cream

5 ml (1 tsp) coffee essence

Caramel

125 g (4 oz) granulated sugar

75 ml (5 tbsp) water

Choux pastry is so easy to make and adaptable for either sweet or savoury dishes. This is a variation on the rather over-used profiterole. The combination of confectioners' custard, lightly flavoured with coffee and a crisp caramel topping makes the whole thing delicious. Those of you who are feeling ambitious should try decorating with spun sugar! The choux buns can be made in advance and either frozen or kept in an airtight tin for a day or so. They will go soggy and will need to be crisped in a hot oven before filling. Prepare the confectioners' custard in advance too, then complete an hour or so before serving.

1. Preheat the combination oven, using only conventional heat, to 200°C.

2. For the buns, place the water and butter in a saucepan on a conventional hob. Bring to the boil and cook until the butter has melted. Sift the flour on to a sheet of greaseproof paper.

3. Remove the saucepan from the heat and immediately shoot in the flour. Beat until the mixture leaves the sides of the pan, if necessary returning to the heat for a few seconds.

4. Allow the mixture to cool slightly, then beat in the eggs, a little at a time, beating well after each addition. The pastry should be smooth and glossy.

5. Place the mixture in a piping bag fitted with a plain nozzle and pipe 18 small buns on to a greased baking dish. (This can be done with a teaspoon if necessary.)

6. Bake the choux buns for about 20 minutes or until well risen and crisp. Slit each bun to allow the steam to escape, then allow to cool. If the buns are to be used immediately, return them to the switched-off oven after slitting and allow them to "dry out" for 5–10 minutes.

7. To make the confectioners' custard, blend a little of the milk with the cornflour, then place with the remaining milk, egg and sugar in a bowl. Whisk thoroughly. Microwave on HIGH for 2 minutes, then whisk thoroughly and microwave for 1 minute more, whisking after 30 seconds. Leave to cool.

8. Whip the cream until stiff, then fold into the cold custard with the coffee essence. Use the mixture to fill the buns, then pile the buns in a pyramid on a serving dish.

9. To make the caramel place the sugar and water in a bowl and microwave on HIGH for 3 minutes. Stir until the sugar has dissolved then return to the oven and microwave on HIGH for 6–7 minutes or until a good caramel colour is reached. Pour the caramel over the buns, leave to cool, then serve.

KIRSCH STREUSEL

SERVES 6–8
•
Pastry

175 g (6 oz) plain flour

75 g (3 oz) butter

25 g (1 oz) caster sugar

1 whole egg, lightly beaten

15–30 ml (1–2 tbsp) water

Filling

2 × 411 g (14½ oz) cans black cherries

30 ml (2 tbsp) kirsch

15 ml (1 tbsp) cornflour

Topping

125 g (4 oz) plain flour

50 g (2 oz) butter

50 g (2 oz) caster sugar

15 g (½ oz) flaked almonds

This streusel recipe can be adapted to use any fruit, but here the cherries, kirsch and almonds complement each other perfectly. It is equally delicious served hot or cold with lashings of whipped cream. The dessert may be prepared well in advance or even the day before a dinner party and either served cold or reheated quickly at the last minute. When making the streusel, allow a little extra time for the pastry to rest and to stone the cherries, which is rather a fiddly job.

1. To make the pastry, sift the flour into a bowl and rub in the butter until the mixture resembles fine breadcrumbs.

2. Stir in the sugar, then lightly mix in the egg and sufficient water to form a dough. Knead lightly. Chill for at least 1 hour.

3. Roll out the pastry and use to line a 23 cm (9 in) flan dish. Prick the base, then bake blind (see Cook's tip, page 97) in a preheated combination oven at 220°C with LOW power microwave for 5 minutes.

4. Drain the cherries, reserving the syrup from 1 can. Stone the cherries, then spread over the pastry case.

5. Microwave the syrup in a glass measuring jug on HIGH for 2 minutes. Blend the kirsch and cornflour together, then stir into the syrup and microwave on HIGH for about 2 minutes, stirring twice or until thickened and smooth. Pour the syrup over the cherries, then set aside.

6. To make the topping, sift the flour into a bowl and rub in the butter until the mixture resembles fine breadcrumbs.

7. Stir in the sugar then spoon over the cherries. Sprinkle over the almonds and bake in a preheated combination oven at 220°C with LOW power microwave for 15 minutes.

AMBROSIA TARTS

MAKES 18

•

50 g (2 oz) raisins, chopped

50 g (2 oz) cut glacé peel, chopped

25 g (1 oz) glacé cherries, chopped

75 g (3 oz) walnuts, chopped

30 ml (2 tbsp) brandy

125 g (4 oz) honey

single cream or Greek yogurt to serve

Pastry

125 g (4 oz) butter, softened

125 g (4 oz) caster sugar

4 egg yolks

2.5 ml (½ tsp) vanilla essence

225 g (8 oz) plain flour

These tarts make a sophisticated dinner party sweet. They are very easy to do and need no last-minute attention. The pastry is a very rich pâte sucrée – delicious for all sorts of tarts – and the filling is an unusual variation on mincemeat. Do not be too generous with the filling in each tart, because it is inclined to leak. Make the filling several days in advance if you have time, and the pastry the day before. The completed tarts will freeze well. Reheat them in the combination oven but do not use microwave power, or they will be soft.

1. Mix the fruit and walnuts in a bowl. Stir in the brandy and microwave on HIGH for 2 minutes.

2. Add the honey and microwave for 2 minutes on HIGH. Leave to cool completely before using.

3. Mix all the pastry ingredients except the flour in a mixer or with a wooden spoon until just combined. Add the flour and knead gently until smooth. Wrap and chill for at least 1 hour.

4. Preheat the combination oven, using only conventional heat, to 200°C. Roll out the pastry and use half to line 18 patty tins. Cut out 18 lids from the remaining pastry. Put a small spoonful of the honey mixture into each tart case and cover with a lid, damping the edges to seal.

5. Bake for about 10–12 minutes or until pale gold in colour. Serve warm with plenty of cream or, better still, Greek strained yoghurt.

OPPOSITE
Midweek special (pages 135–138); Smoked haddock pâté; Chicken Italienne and Potatoes with garlic and parsley; Peas in the French way; Poires au grenadine.

OVERLEAF
Vegetarian à la carte (pages 132–134); Peperonata with Greek yogurt and Wheaten soda farl; Aubergines stuffed with walnuts; Banoffy pie.

ICED APRICOT AND MARZIPAN JALOUSIE

SERVES 6
•

225 g (8 oz) puff pastry (frozen is fine)

1 × 330 g (12 oz) can apricots in natural juice, well drained

125 g (4 oz) marzipan

125 g (4 oz) icing sugar

about 30 ml (2 tbsp) water

 This is a recipe that we have made in demonstrations for a long time. It is very quick and easy to make but doesn't taste it! It is useful to keep the ingredients in the larder to make up for unexpected guests or for a family treat.

1. Divide the pastry in half and roll each half out to a rectangle 15 × 30 cm (6 × 12 in).

2. Put one piece on a dampened baking sheet suitable for your combination oven. Arrange the drained apricot halves, cut side up, on the top leaving a clear border all round.

3. Put a small ball of marzipan into each apricot half.

4. Fold the remaining piece of pastry in half lengthways and with a sharp knife cut from the fold towards the edge leaving 1 cm (½ in) uncut at the edge. Repeat at 1 cm (½ in) intervals. Unfold the pastry and lay it over the base, damping the edges to seal them.

5. Scallop the edges of the jalousie, and bake in a preheated combination oven at 220°C with LOW power microwave for 12–16 minutes or until golden.

6. Mix the icing sugar with a little water to make a thick glacé icing. Drizzle this over the jalousie. Serve warm, cut into slices.

PREVIOUS PAGE
Chicken liver mousse with green peppercorns (page 31); Turbane of whiting (page 40) with Duchesse potatoes (page 80) and buttered green beans; Kirsch streusel (page 102).

OPPOSITE
Canapes (pages 111–117); From top to bottom: Chicken and mushroom filled choux buns; Cheese balls; Mini plaits; Clafoutis; Cheese and mint triangles; Mini quiches; Salmon boats; Crostini.

LES TROIS SORBETS
(lime, orange and raspberry sorbets)

SERVES 8
•
Lime Sorbet

225 g (8 oz) caster sugar

200 ml (7 fl oz) water

grated rind and juice of 3 limes

grated rind and juice of 1 lemon

2 egg whites

Orange Sorbet

125 g (4 oz) caster sugar

175 ml (6 fl oz) water

1 × 170 ml (6 fl oz) carton
concentrated frozen orange juice

2 egg whites

Raspberry Sorbet

225 g (8 oz) caster sugar

175 ml (6 fl oz) water

450 g (1 lb) raspberries, puréed
and sieved

2 egg whites

This dessert arose after we visited a very expensive restaurant where one of the desserts was Les Trois Sorbets. Since that date it has been served frequently at home and it never fails to please. Visually it is very pretty, and because it can be made up to 6 weeks in advance, it is a boon to the busy hostess.

All sorbets are made by the same method:

1. Microwave the sugar and water together on HIGH for 2 minutes. Stir until all the sugar has dissolved, then microwave the syrup on HIGH for 3 minutes, without stirring.

2. Add the purée, or juice and rinds to the syrup and leave to cool.

3. When cool, freeze. The lime sorbet will need straining first.

4. When the syrup is frozen turn it into a mixer bowl or food processor and beat well. Return the mixture to the freezer and then repeat when frozen.

5. Beat the egg whites until stiff and fold into the beaten ice mixture.

6. Freeze until required. Twenty minutes before serving transfer the sorbets from the freezer to the refrigerator to allow them to soften slightly.

7. Serve a small scoop of each sorbet on each plate. Garnish with fresh mint leaves and accompany with Tuiles (see page 92).

CANAPÉS AND PETITS FOURS

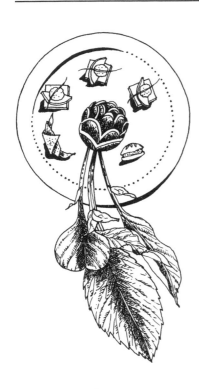

*I*T IS OFTEN the little touches which make your entertaining memorable. Next time don't open a bag of crisps or nuts, but instead make a canapé or two to serve before the meal. If you are really organised, you could keep a store of mini quiches or cheese and mint triangles in the freezer, ready to bring out and reheat before a dinner party.

As canapés can be a little fiddly to prepare, it is easier to make a larger quantity and store them for later. We find they are ideal for children's teas.

Canapés are usually cooked using only conventional heat. This is because they are so small they would not benefit from combination cooking.

There are occasions when you want to entertain a lot of people without sitting them down to a meal. An early evening or lunchtime drinks party is the ideal solution. Allow approximately 8 canapés per person, and choose a mixture of hot and cold for ease of serving. Serve a selection attractively arranged on trays or platters. In an emergency, a clean oven tray covered with doylies will serve.

Without a doubt, nibbling a petit four with your coffee puts the finishing touch to a meal. Homemade ones are best of all and will leave your guests with the lasting impression that no effort has been spared on their behalf. When presented in a gift box, home-made sweets also make ideal presents for special friends. All are simple to make using the micro-wave facility on your combination oven.

CHICKEN AND MUSHROOM FILLED CHOUX BUNS

MAKES 24
•
Choux Pastry

150 ml (5 fl oz) water

50 g (2 oz) butter

65 g (2½ oz) plain flour

2 eggs (size 3), lightly beaten

Filling

25 g (1 oz) butter

1 very small onion, finely chopped

50 g (2 oz) mushrooms, wiped and finely chopped

25 g (1 oz) plain flour

250 ml (8 fl oz) milk

75 g (3 oz) cooked chicken, finely chopped

salt and freshly ground black pepper

These delicious little buns are equally good with a sweet or savoury filling. They make ideal cocktail savouries as they can be made in any size and can have a wide range of fillings. We give a recipe for a chicken and mushroom filling, but any filling suitable for vol-au-vent may be used. Alternatively, keep it simple by using a cream cheese. The buns freeze successfully unfilled but will be soggy when defrosted. This can easily be remedied by crisping for a few minutes in a hot oven before filling.

1. To make the pastry, place the water and butter in a saucepan on a conventional hob. Bring to the boil and cook until the butter has melted. Sift the flour on to a sheet of greaseproof paper.

2. Remove the saucepan from the heat and immediately shoot in the flour. Beat until the mixture leaves the sides of the pan, if necessary returning to the heat for a few seconds.

3. Allow the mixture to cool slightly, then beat in the eggs, a little at a time, beating well after each addition. The pastry should be smooth and glossy. Preheat the combination oven, using only conventional heat, to 200°C.

4. Place the choux pastry mixture in a piping bag fitted with a plain nozzle and pipe 24 small buns on to greased baking dishes. This can be done with a teaspoon, if necessary.

5. Bake the buns for about 20 minutes or until well risen and golden brown. In most ovens, this will need to be done in 2 batches.

6. Slit each bun to allow the steam to escape, then allow to cool. If the buns go soggy, crisp for a few minutes in a hot oven before filling.

7. To make the filling, microwave the butter in a bowl on HIGH for 1 minute. Stir in the onion and mushrooms, and microwave on HIGH for 2 minutes.

8. Stir in the flour, then gradually blend in the milk. Microwave on HIGH for 2 minutes, beat thoroughly, then microwave for a further 2 minutes, beating again at the end of the cooking time.

9. Stir in the chicken, then season to taste. If the mixture is too thick, add a little extra milk and reheat.

10. When the filling has cooled, split the choux buns in half, and fill each with a teaspoon of the mixture.

CHEESE AND MINT TRIANGLES

MAKES 24

•

75 g (3 oz) butter

8 sheets filo pastry

Filling

25 g (1 oz) butter

25 g (1 oz) plain flour

250 ml (8 fl oz) milk

125 g (4 oz) feta or Cheshire cheese, grated

15 ml (1 tbsp) fresh mint, chopped

1 egg

salt and freshly ground black pepper

These are based on a Greek recipe, where feta cheese is traditionally used in the filling. We find that Cheshire cheese works very well if feta is not available. The triangles can be prepared in advance and frozen uncooked. They can be cooked from frozen, but will take slightly longer.

1. First make the filling: place the butter in a bowl, and microwave on HIGH for 1 minute until melted. Stir in the flour, then gradually blend in the milk. Microwave on HIGH for 4 minutes, whisking halfway through the cooking time and again on completion.

2. Beat the cheese, mint, egg and seasoning into the sauce, then leave to cool.

3. For the pastry, microwave the butter on HIGH for 1 minute until melted. Open out the pastry sheets and cut each one lengthways into 3. Preheat the combination oven, using only conventional heat, to 220°C.

4. Brush a strip of filo pastry with butter. Place 5 ml (1 tsp) of the filling at the end of the strip. Fold the strip over on itself to form a triangle enclosing the filling. Continue to fold the pastry over on itself, adding a layer of filo to the triangle each time, until you reach the end of the strip of filo.

5. Repeat with the rest of the pastry strips. It is important to work quickly or the pastry will dry out and become brittle. To prevent this, cover unused pastry with a damp tea towel.

6. Brush the triangles with melted butter, place on a greased baking dish and cook for 10–12 minutes or until crisp and golden brown. Serve warm.

MINI QUICHES

•

Pastry

---

225 g (8 oz) plain flour

---

salt

---

50 g (2 oz) margarine

---

50 g (2 oz) lard or white fat

---

45 ml (3 tbsp) cold water

Filling

---

5 ml (1 tsp) butter

---

125 g (4 oz) smoked bacon, finely chopped

---

125 g (4 oz) onion, finely chopped

---

125 g (4 oz) Cheddar cheese, finely grated

---

2 eggs

---

300 ml (½ pt) milk

---

salt and freshly ground black pepper

 These mini quiches are simple to make and easy for your guests to eat without too many crumbs. The quiches can be frozen, stacked between sheets of greaseproof paper, but they must be reheated to serve or the pastry will be a little wet. Vary the filling, using about 350 g (12 oz) of filling per 24 quiches. Our favourites include smoked haddock or ham and asparagus.

1. Sift the flour and salt into a bowl then rub in the fat until the mixture resembles fine breadcrumbs.

2. Stir in the water, then knead together lightly to form a soft dough.

3. Roll out the pastry on a floured board and cut out 24 rounds with a 7.5 cm (3 in) cutter. Use to line bun tins.

4. For the filling, microwave the butter in a bowl on HIGH for 30 seconds. Add the bacon and onion and microwave on HIGH for 4 minutes, stirring halfway through the cooking time.

5. Place a teaspoon of the filling in each pastry case. Cover with a teaspoon of cheese. Preheat the combination oven, using only conventional heat, to 200°C.

6. In a large jug, beat the eggs with the milk and season with salt and pepper. Pour a little into each flan case.

7. Bake the quiches in two batches for about 20 minutes or until golden brown. Serve hot or cold.

MINI PLAITS

MAKES 24

•

450 g (1 lb) puff pastry

225 g (8 oz) low-fat sausage meat

1 small onion, finely chopped

50 g (2 oz) mushrooms, wiped and finely chopped

15 ml (1 tbsp) tomato chutney

dash of Worcestershire sauce

salt and freshly ground black pepper

1 egg, beaten

 These little plaits always go very quickly at cocktail parties. They are really an upmarket sausage roll but the addition of mushrooms and chutney makes them rather special. They can be frozen before or after cooking and are best served hot.

1. Cut the pastry in half, then roll out each half to approximately 40 × 30 cm (16 × 12 in). Trim the edges then cut each half into 12 squares.

2. Mix together all the remaining ingredients, binding with half of the egg.

3. Place a teaspoon of the mixture down the centre third of each pastry square, leaving a plain border at the top and bottom. Using a sharp knife, cut 3 diagonal slits down each side of the pastry square, on either side of the filling.

4. Brush the edges with egg, fold in the top and plait the strips over the filling. Tuck under the bottom. Repeat with all the pastry squares. Preheat the combination oven, using only conventional heat, to 200°C.

5. Place the plaits on a baking dish, brush with the remaining egg and bake in two batches for 15–18 minutes or until golden brown. Serve hot.

SALMON BOATS

MAKES 24

•

125 g (4 oz) wholemeal self-raising flour

125 g (4 oz) plain flour

salt

50 g (2 oz) margarine

50 g (2 oz) lard or white fat

45 ml (3 tbsp) water

1 quantity Smoked salmon mousse (see page 32)

To Garnish

small rolls of smoked salmon

fresh parsley sprigs

tiny pieces of lemon peel

The little boat-shaped moulds are a bit tricky to line and in this recipe need to be baked blind. They can, however be prepared well in advance and frozen without the filling, then assembled at the last minute. Fill with any savoury sauce-based mixture. The boats may also be filled with a little confectioners' custard and fresh fruit for a dessert.

1. Place the flours and salt in a bowl and rub in the fat until the mixture resembles fine breadcrumbs.

2. Stir in the water, then knead together lightly to form a soft dough.

3. Roll out the pastry on a floured board and use to line 24 boat-shaped moulds. Preheat the combination oven, using only conventional heat, to 200°C.

4. Place a small piece of foil in the centre of each pastry case, then bake blind for 10 minutes. Remove the foil and bake for a further 5 minutes.

5. Remove from the tins and cool. To serve, fill with salmon mousse and garnish with smoked salmon, parsley and lemon peel. Serve cold.

CLAFOUTIS

MAKES ABOUT 16
•
125 g (4 oz) Cheddar cheese

300 ml (½ pt) milk

2 eggs

50 g (2 oz) plain flour

salt and freshly ground black pepper

oil (see method)

 These are savoury Yorkshire puddings which are delicious hot. They do need to be served straight from the oven or they will collapse and go rather soggy. We have used cheese, but other ingredients such as prawns or mushrooms and bacon could be used. Allow the batter to stand for 1 hour for best results.

1. Finely grate half the cheese. Cut the rest into tiny cubes. Set aside.

2. Combine the milk, eggs and flour in a blender or food processor and blend until smooth. Pour the batter into a jug and beat in the grated cheese. Leave to stand for 1 hour. Preheat the combination oven, using only conventional heat, to 200°C.

3. Place a little oil in each of 16 bun tins, and heat in the preheated oven for 5 minutes.

4. Pour the batter into the tins and sprinkle over the cheese cubes. Return to the oven and bake at 200°C for 15–20 minutes or until well risen and golden brown.

5. Remove from the tins and serve hot.

CROSTINI

MAKES 24
•
4 large slices medium-sliced bread

25 g (1 oz) butter

1 clove garlic, crushed

freshly ground black pepper

Topping

1 × 50 g (2 oz) can anchovy fillets

1 tinned pimiento, drained and cut into 24 strips

25 g (1 oz) cream cheese

 These are garlic-flavoured croutons which are simple to make in a variety of shapes with any number of different toppings. We have chosen a pimiento and anchovy topping which looks colourful on the cocktail table, but soft cheeses or pâtés can also be used.

1. Cut the crusts off the bread, then, using a 5 cm (2 in) round cutter, cut 6 moon shapes from each slice.

2. Microwave the butter in a bowl on LOW for 1 minute to soften. Beat in the garlic and black pepper. Preheat the combination oven, using only conventional heat, to 220°C.

3. Spread the butter over the moon shapes and bake for 10 minutes or until crisp.

4. Top each crouton with a strip of anchovy and a strip of pimiento. Pipe a small rosette of cheese at each end, if necessary softening the cheese first with a little milk. Serve cold.

CHEESE BALLS

MAKES ABOUT 30
•
50 g (2 oz) butter

225 g (8 oz) Gouda cheese, finely grated

5 ml (1 tsp) mustard

15–30 ml (1–2 tbsp) single cream

freshly ground black pepper

To Coat
Choose one of the following:

25 g (1 oz) ham, finely chopped

25 g (1 oz) nuts, finely chopped

45 ml (3 tbsp) chopped fresh parsley

 Serve these colourful cheese balls on sticks for easy eating. The mixture, potted cheese coated with parsley, ham or nuts, may be prepared in advance and the cheese balls stored in the refrigerator for up to 24 hours.

1. Microwave the butter in a bowl on LOW power for 1 minute to soften. Beat in the next four ingredients.

2. Roll the mixture into small balls, then roll in one of the coatings. Chill before serving skewered on cocktail sticks.

—— COOK'S TIP——

As an alternative coating, why not try paprika or poppy seeds.

STILTON TART

SERVES 4
•
1 × 275 g (10 oz) packet of bread mix

225 g (8 oz) Stilton cheese

120 ml (4 fl oz) single cream

2 eggs, beaten

freshly ground black pepper

This is particularly useful as a way of using up the leftover Stilton after Christmas, or later in the year if you have frozen the cheese. Use this as an informal supper dish, as an accompaniment to Watercress soup (see page 22) or cut in small pieces as a cocktail savoury. While this is best straight from the oven it may successfully be reheated in a hot oven, and it freezes well.

1. Make up the bread mix following the directions on the packet.

2. Divide the kneaded dough in half and roll each piece out to a 25 cm (10 in) circle. Place on 2 greased trays suitable for your oven. Leave to rise while you make the filling.

3. Crumble the cheese into a bowl. Stir in the cream and beaten eggs and season to taste.

4. When the dough rounds have begun to rise at the edges put the filling into the centre of each circle of dough leaving a space around the rim to keep the filling in.

5. Bake in a preheated combination oven at maximum heat with LOW power microwave for 10–12 minutes or until golden.

PEPPERMINT CREAMS

MAKES ABOUT 24
•
225 g (8 oz) icing sugar

1 egg white

peppermint essence

green food colouring

50 g (2 oz) plain chocolate

Peppermints are the sweet most often served at the end of a meal, probably because peppermint is thought to aid digestion. These sweets are very simple to make, but taste and look impressive. The chocolate decoration can be as simple or elaborate as you like. The sweets need 24 hours to dry out and will keep in an airtight container for up to 1 week.

1. Sift the icing sugar into a bowl. Beat in enough egg white to form a stiff, malleable paste.

2. Add a few drops of peppermint essence to taste. Divide the mixture in half. Set one half aside and add a little green food colouring to the rest.

3. Knead each peppermint mixture together lightly. Lightly dust a clean work surface with icing sugar and roll out the peppermint to about 5 mm (¼ in) thick.

4. Cut out 2.5 cm (1 in) rounds, then leave the peppermints to dry out for 24 hours.

5. When the peppermints are dry, microwave the chocolate in a bowl on HIGH for 1 minute. Stir until completely melted.

6. Dip some of the mints in chocolate, or use a greaseproof piping bag to pipe designs on top of them.

FRESH CREAM TRUFFLES AND COLLETTES

MAKES ABOUT 15

•

Collettes

225 g (8 oz) plain chocolate

30 ml (2 tbsp) double cream

15 g (½ oz) unsalted butter

15 ml (1 tbsp) rum or Cointreau

about 15 paper sweet cases

To finish as Truffles

cocoa powder or

175 g (6 oz) white chocolate or

125 g (4 oz) plain chocolate

Both of us are great fans of Belgian chocolates. However, these are not always easy to obtain so we resolved to make our own. Our chocolates are considerably cheaper and almost as good and are very popular as presents or at the end of a meal. The recipe below will make several types of chocolate if you alter the presentation. The choice includes collettes (chocolate cups with piped truffle filling), cocoa-rolled truffles, white chocolate dipped truffles and dark chocolate dipped truffles. Prepare in advance of when you need them as they are rather messy to make. They will keep in a cool place for about a week if you hide them well!

1. To make the collettes, microwave 50 g (2 oz) of the chocolate on HIGH for 2 minutes until melted. Using a paint brush, coat the inside of the sweet cases with chocolate. If you have time, repeat when set so there are two coats in each sweet case.

2. Put the remaining 175 g (6 oz) plain chocolate in a bowl with the cream and microwave on HIGH for 2 minutes; stir and microwave on HIGH for a further minute or until melted.

3. Beat in the butter, rum or Cointreau. Cool by standing the bowl in cold water, stirring constantly until it begins to set. Working quickly transfer all the mixture to a piping bag with a 1 cm (½ in) star nozzle.

4. Pipe stars of the mixture into the chocolate cases and leave to set.

5. For the truffles, pipe the mixture directly on to greaseproof paper through a plain nozzle to make balls about the size of a small walnut. (This is much less messy than using spoons!) Chill thoroughly. When the mixture is almost set powder your hands with a little cocoa powder and roll it into balls (this is messy!).

6. Coat the truffles: either roll in extra cocoa powder or dip in melted white or plain chocolate. Use a couple of skewers to help you with this and make sure the truffles are well chilled.

7. Decorate with a little contrasting chocolate if desired and place in sweet cases.

FUDGE

MAKES ABOUT 40 SQUARES

•

50 g (2 oz) butter

450 g (1 lb) caster sugar

1 × 411 g (14½ oz) can evaporated milk

 Once this is made, you will have difficulty keeping it, as it is delicious! It is so simple to make in the microwave and has become a firm family favourite. We love it plain, but do try adding dried fruit, nuts, crystallised ginger or chocolate.

1. Lightly grease and line the base of an 18 × 23 cm (7 × 9 in) baking tin with non-stick silicone paper.

2. Mix the sugar, milk and remaining butter in a large deep bowl and micro-wave on HIGH for 5 minutes. Stir until the sugar has dissolved.

3. Return to the microwave and boil on HIGH for 15–17 minutes or until the "soft ball" stage is reached (see Cook's tip).

4. Beat the mixture until thick and creamy, then pour into the prepared tin. Leave to set before cutting into squares.

—— COOK'S TIP——

The fudge is ready to set when a teaspoon of the hot mixture dropped into a cup of cold water forms a soft ball.

COCONUT ICE

MAKES ABOUT 30 CUBES

•

5 ml (1 tsp) butter

150 ml (5 fl oz) milk

450 g (1 lb) caster sugar

150 g (5 oz) desiccated coconut

red food colouring

Although not everyone's favourite, this colourful sweet is good to serve as part of an arrangement of petit fours. With the aid of the microwave the coconut ice is easy to make. If in doubt about the setting point of the milk syrup, drop a teaspoonful into a bowl of cold water. It should form a very soft ball. Do not let the syrup go too far, or it will set before you have time to colour half of it.

1. With the butter, grease and line the base of an 18 cm (7 in) square baking tin with non-stick silicone paper.

2. Pour the milk into a large bowl and stir in the sugar. Microwave on HIGH for 5 minutes, then stir until the sugar has dissolved.

3. Return to the microwave and heat on HIGH for 2 minutes, then on LOW for 8–10 minutes or until the setting point as described above is reached.

4. Stir in the coconut, then pour half the mixture into the prepared tin. Quickly add a few drops of colouring to the remaining mixture and pour over the top. Leave to set before cutting into squares.

MENUS À LA CARTE

OCCASIONALLY IT IS a good idea to let someone else do the planning for you, and in this section we have done just that with a set of menus that work for various occasions, from the very romantic dinner for 2 to the more informal Indian or Chinese menu.

Here, you will find a menu for a complete Christmas dinner with a difference, a traditional afternoon tea and a meal suitable for vegetarians. Then if you feel really decadent how about the champagne breakfast; try to find an excuse for this one and when the purse begins to feel empty we have a midweek special menu so you can still impress without spending a lot.

Most of the menus have been photographed so that you can see exactly what you can accomplish. The hardest task will be to decide who is going to be lucky enough to share these lovely occasions with you!

INDIAN

TANDOORI SCAMPI

POPPADOMS

SAAG GOSHT

RICE

MUNG DHAL

KACHOOMBAR

*I*T CAN BE fun to make a complete Indian meal for guests, although it is worth checking that they will enjoy the spicy food before you begin to cook. We have found that Indian cooking is becoming more popular; indeed the courses run for us at the Contemporary Cookery School by Rafi Fernandez book up quickly.

Indian food is ideal for entertaining as it needs little last-minute attention and indeed will benefit if cooked the day before and left for the flavours to develop. All you need to complete this meal is plain boiled rice (for cooking instructions see page 128). If you want a dessert offer one or two of the sorbets (see page 88).

TANDOORI SCAMPI

SERVES 4
•
450 g (1 lb) frozen unbreaded scampi

150 ml (5 fl oz) natural yogurt

grated rind of 1 lemon

5 ml (1 tsp) ground ginger

5 ml (1 tsp) chilli powder

5 ml (1 tsp) ground coriander

2.5 ml (½ tsp) ground cumin

1 clove garlic, crushed

5 ml (1 tsp) tomato purée

salt and freshly ground black pepper

The tandoori sauce is simple to make and can be used to cook chicken or fish. Ideally, king prawns should be used for this recipe, but as these are not always easily available and are very expensive we have used scampi. This is still not cheap but does make a delicious addition to an Indian meal.

1. Defrost the scampi (see chart, page 157) and drain thoroughly.

2. Mix all the remaining ingredients together in a shallow bowl and stir in the scampi. Cover and marinate in the refrigerator for 3–4 hours.

3. Microwave on HIGH for 6 minutes, stirring halfway through the cooking time.

SAAG GOSHT

SERVES 4
•

450 g (1 lb) braising steak

45 ml (3 tbsp) sunflower oil

1 clove garlic, crushed

2.5 cm (1 in) piece of fresh ginger, grated

225 g (8 oz) onions, chopped

10 ml (2 tsp) garam masala

5 ml (1 tsp) ground coriander

5 ml (1 tsp) turmeric

3 small dried chillies (or to taste)

225 g (8 oz) leaf spinach, frozen or fresh

3 tomatoes, sliced

5 ml (1 tsp) tomato purée

300 ml (½ pt) water

2.5 ml (½ tsp) salt

This is a rich tender vegetable stew cooked in half the normal time in the combination oven. Do make it the day before you need it if possible so that the flavours really have time to develop. Garnish it with some fresh coriander leaves if they are available.

1. Cube the meat and fry in the oil in a large frying pan on a conventional hob until brown all over.

2. With a slotted spoon transfer the meat to a large casserole. Add the garlic, ginger and onions to the oil remaining in the pan and fry for 2 minutes.

3. Add the spices, removing the seeds from the chillies if you don't want the dish to be too hot. Stir well for 3 minutes.

4. Add the vegetables and spice mixture to the meat, with the spinach (see Cook's tip), tomatoes, tomato purée, water and salt. Cover the casserole with a tight fitting lid, suitable for convection cooking.

5. Cook in a preheated combination oven at 160°C with LOW power microwave for 1 hour, stirring halfway through. When the dish is ready, the meat should be tender and most of the liquid should have been absorbed.

—— COOK'S TIP——

If you use fresh spinach you will have trouble fitting it into your casserole. To make it more manageable, wash it thoroughly and place the leaves with the water adhering to them, in a large bowl. Microwave on HIGH for 2 minutes. The wilted spinach will be easier to handle.

RICE

Rice is easily cooked in a combination oven using the microwave alone. Simply measure the rice allowing ½ a teacup per person, rinse it and place in a large bowl with a little salt and double the quantity of boiling water, e.g. To serve 4, 2 cups of rice, 4 cups of boiling water and 5 ml (1 tsp) salt.

Microwave uncovered on HIGH for 12 minutes stirring once. Remove from the oven and cover for 5–10 minutes before serving. All the water should be absorbed and the rice will be separate and fluffy.

MUNG DHAL

Mung beans are more familiar when grown as bean sprouts, but the beans themselves are also good to use. They cook quickly and have the advantage of being able to be cooked without soaking. They can be cooked in the microwave but as it is a good idea to boil them fiercely for 10 minutes at the start of cooking, it may be easier to do this on the hob. Serve with rice as a meal on its own or as part of a complete Indian meal. Mung dhal benefits from being made the day before it is required and reheated to serve.

SERVES 4

225 g (8 oz) mung beans

30 ml (2 tbsp) oil

1 large onion, chopped

2 cloves garlic, crushed

5 ml (1 tsp) ground cumin

5 ml (1 tsp) turmeric

1.25 ml (¼ tsp) chilli powder

salt and freshly ground black pepper

deep fried onion, to garnish (see page 20)

1. Place the beans in a saucepan on the hob, add cold water to cover and bring to the boil. Boil for 10 minutes then lower the heat and simmer for 30–40 minutes or until the beans are softened.

2. Place the oil in a casserole and stir in the onion and garlic. Microwave on HIGH for 4 minutes, then stir in the spices and microwave on HIGH for 2 minutes.

3. Drain the cooked beans, stir into the onion and spice mixture and season with salt and pepper.

4. Reheat in the microwave on HIGH for 3–4 minutes before serving and garnish with the deep fried onion.

KACHOOMBAR

This recipe comes from our good friend Rafi Fernandez, who is well known as an authority on Indian and Malay cooking. It is a delicious and cooling salad to accompany an Indian meal.

SERVES 4

1 large onion, finely chopped

4 small firm tomatoes, finely chopped

2 fresh green chillies, seeded and finely chopped

15 ml (1 tbsp) fresh coriander and mint leaves, chopped

juice of 1 lemon

salt

5 ml (1 tsp) sugar

1. Mix all the ingredients in a bowl, cover and chill for at least 1 hour before serving.

CHINESE

A CHINESE MEAL is colourful and nutritious and can quickly create a party atmosphere if chopsticks are used. Serve a selection of dishes at the same time. Every guest should have a small bowl and can help themselves to rice and whatever else takes their fancy.

Traditionally Chinese food is rapidly stir-fried over a high heat in a wok. In these days of ceramic hobs or solid hot plates it can be difficult getting a wok to heat up sufficiently, so we have put together some recipes suitable for your combination oven.

It can be difficult getting all the dishes for a Chinese meal cooked at the same time. By using a wok in conjunction with your combination oven it is easy to produce a complete Chinese meal. The menu below serves 6, with the addition of fresh fruit for dessert and China tea.

CHINESE SPARE RIBS

SERVES 4–6
•
1 kg (2¼ lb) pork spare ribs

30 ml (2 tbsp) dry sherry

30 ml (2 tbsp) soy sauce

2.5 ml (½ teaspoon) red food colouring

45 ml (3 tbsp) brown sugar

45 ml (3 tbsp) hoisin sauce

10 ml (2 tsp) Chinese five spice powder

3 cloves garlic, crushed

These tasty spare ribs may be served as part of a Chinese meal. We also find they are a great favourite with our children as a supper dish; we think the popularity stems from the fact they can pretend to be cavemen and eat with their fingers! The cooking time has been based on fairly meaty ribs. If yours are not terribly well covered reduce the cooking time. For the best results, marinate the ribs for 24 hours.

1. Cut the spare ribs into individual ribs, and trim.

2. Mix the remaining ingredients together in a large glass bowl, add all the ribs and coat with the mixture. Marinate for at least two hours, preferably overnight.

3. With kitchen tongs, transfer the ribs to a large shallow dish. Reserve the marinade. Cook the ribs in a preheated combination oven at 220°C with LOW power microwave for 20 minutes, turning over halfway through cooking.

4. Drain the cooking juices from the ribs into the bowl containing the reserved marinade. Mix and microwave on HIGH for 4 minutes or until boiling rapidly.

5. Serve the ribs with the sauce poured over.

CHA SHAO
(HONEY ROAST PORK)

SERVES 4
•
15 ml (1 tbsp) dry sherry

30 ml (2 tbsp) runny honey

30 ml (2 tbsp) soy sauce

15 ml (1 tbsp) hoisin sauce

10 ml (2 tsp) sesame oil

2 pork fillets

Cha Shao, the basis of many Chinese dishes, is marvellously easy in a combination oven. The result is perfectly cooked but not dried up. We suggest serving it with bean sprouts, but traditionally it is served as part of rice with mixed meats. It is also delicious cold, sliced with a salad or hot with a barbecue sauce, jacket potatoes and a salad.

1. Mix the first 5 ingredients in a large glass bowl, add the meat and marinate for at least 2 hours, preferably overnight.

2. Drain the pork and place on a rack over a roasting dish. Cook in a preheated combination oven at 220°C with LOW power microwave for 20 minutes.

3. Use 225 g (8 oz) as directed in the following recipe, and freeze the remainder.

CHA SHAO WITH BEAN SPROUTS

SERVES 4
•
30 ml (2 tbsp) sunflower oil

1 onion, sliced

1 × 175 g (6 oz) pack bean sprouts

15 ml (1 tbsp) soy sauce

225 g (8 oz) cooked cha shao (see previous recipe)

1. Combine the oil and onion in a large bowl and microwave on HIGH for 2 minutes.

2. Stir in the bean sprouts and microwave on HIGH for 2 minutes.

3. Add the soy sauce and mix well. Season and cook on HIGH for 2 minutes more.

4. Thinly slice the pork and microwave on HIGH for 1 minute.

5. Transfer the bean sprouts to a hot serving dish and top with the thinly sliced pork. Serve at once.

CHINESE BEEF WITH PEPPERS, MUSHROOMS AND CASHEW NUTS

SERVES 4 AS PART OF A MEAL

•

Marinade

15 ml (1 tbsp) dark soy sauce
15 ml (1 tbsp) dry sherry
5 ml (1 tsp) sugar
15 ml (1 tbsp) oil
15 ml (1 tbsp) cornflour

Chinese Beef

225 g (8 oz) rump steak
25 g (1 oz) wood ears (optional)
15 ml (1 tbsp) oil
1½ red pepper, seeded and sliced
125 g (4 oz) button mushrooms, wiped and halved
125 g (4 oz) cashew nuts

 As with most Chinese recipes, this is extremely quick to prepare. The beef is so tender it melts in the mouth and contrasts well with the crispness of the cashew nuts. This recipe can be cooked in advance and reheated quickly at the last minute. Do not add the cashew nuts until you are ready to serve.

1. Prepare the marinade by mixing all the ingredients in a glass bowl. Slice the steak into thin strips and stir into the marinade. Marinate for 20 minutes.

2. If wood ears are used, soak them in hot water for 20 minutes, then drain and rinse in fresh water. Slice thinly.

3. Place the oil in a bowl and microwave on HIGH for 1 minute. Stir in the meat and marinade. Microwave on HIGH for 2 minutes, stirring after 1 minute.

4. Stir in the vegetables and microwave on HIGH for 2 minutes, then stir in the nuts and serve.

MANGE TOUT WITH WATER CHESTNUTS

SERVE 4 AS PART OF A MEAL

•

15 ml (1 tbsp) groundnut oil

30 ml (2 tbsp) spring onions, chopped

225 g (8 oz) mange tout, trimmed

15 ml (1 tbsp) light soy sauce

a pinch of sugar

15 ml (1 tbsp) sesame oil

1 × 230 g (8¼ oz) can water chestnuts, drained and sliced

 Mange tout, spring onions and water chestnuts combine to make a delicious vegetable dish which is as crisp as it is colourful. It complements the rest of the Chinese meal perfectly.

1. Place the oil in a casserole, stir in the spring onions and mange tout, cover and microwave on HIGH for 3 minutes.

2. Stir in the remaining ingredients, cover and microwave on HIGH for a further 2 minutes. Serve at once.

CHAMPAGNE BREAKFAST

*SMOKED HADDOCK SOUFFLÉ
OMELETTE*

WALNUT BRIOCHE

LEMON CURD

*STRAWBERRY JAM WITH
COINTREAU*

E VERY SO OFTEN it is important to be totally self-indulgent and a meal like this is ideal. Although it is called a breakfast, it isn't intended to be eaten at 7 o'clock in the morning, when your eyes are just open. Save it for brunch time. It can be a great way to entertain, although it may be inclined to drift on into the afternoon, and makes a refreshing change from lunch and dinner parties. Start off with the smoked haddock soufflé omelette and go on to walnut brioche toast with fresh preserves. Accompany it with plenty of freshly-squeezed orange juice and champagne and when you feel you have had enough, serve the coffee.

SMOKED HADDOCK SOUFFLÉ OMELETTE

SERVES 2

•

15 g (½ oz) butter

2 large eggs, separated

30 ml (2 tbsp) milk

freshly ground black pepper

*125 g (4 oz) smoked haddock,
skinned and thinly sliced*

50 g (2 oz) Jarlsberg cheese, sliced

This is an ideal breakfast dish requiring very little thought and effort. If the omelette were cooked on the hob, cooked haddock would be required for the filling. Using the microwave means you can cook both the fish and the omelette in one simple action, but if the fish is frozen it will need to be skinned and defrosted on LOW for 2 minutes before use.

1. Put the butter into a 20 cm (8 in) china or glass flan dish and microwave on HIGH power for 30 seconds to melt. Tilt the dish so that it is completely coated in butter.

2. Beat the egg yolks and milk together in a bowl and add black pepper to taste.

3. Whisk the egg whites until they are stiff; fold into the yolk mixture.

4. Pour the egg mixture into the prepared flan dish and top with the thinly sliced haddock and the cheese.

5. Microwave on HIGH for 4 minutes, turning halfway, or until the fish flakes and the omelette is nearly set.

6. Flash the omelette under a very hot grill until the edges are brown, and serve at once.

WALNUT BRIOCHE

MAKES 2
•
675 g (1½ lb) strong bread flour

5 ml (1 tsp) salt

10 ml (2 tsp) baking powder

50 g (2 oz) caster sugar

1 sachet easy blend dried yeast

175 g (6 oz) butter, softened

300 ml (½ pt) milk

2 large eggs

125 g (4 oz) walnuts, chopped

Home-made bread for breakfast is always appreciated, although not many of us get up early enough to make it fresh. This is the next best thing. Make it the night before and toast it in the morning – the walnuts will be especially delicious. Serve with unsalted or very slightly salted butter and strawberry jam for a Continental flavour.

1. Sift the flour, salt and baking powder into a bowl. Add the sugar and yeast and stir well.

2. Add the butter and warm milk (see Cook's tip). Stir in the eggs and mix well until all the liquid has been incorporated. Knead well for about 5 minutes, either with a mixer or by hand. If the mixture is too sticky add a little extra flour.

3. Knead in the chopped walnuts and divide the dough in half. Knead each half separately and place in two 18 cm (7 in) greased tins or dishes or brioche tins (if these are permitted in your oven). A 23 × 13 cm (9 × 5 in) loaf tin will do just as well.

4. Loosely cover the bread and leave to rise until doubled in bulk (about 1 hour).

5. Bake in a preheated combination oven at 200°C with LOW power micro-wave for 12–15 minutes until golden. The bread should sound hollow when tapped on the base. Cool on a wire rack, and eat warm or toasted.

—— COOK'S TIP——

Soften the butter in the microwave on HIGH for 45 seconds – 1 minute. It should be just on the point of melting. Warm the milk by microwaving in a measuring jug to blood heat.

LEMON CURD

MAKES ABOUT 575 g 1¼ lb)
•
125 g (4 oz) unsalted butter

grated rind and juice of 3 large lemons

225 g (8 oz) caster sugar

3 eggs, beaten

1. Combine the butter, lemon rind and juice in a large mixing bowl and micro-wave on HIGH for 3 minutes or until the butter melts.

2. Stir in the sugar and microwave on HIGH for 2 minutes.

3. Stir again to dissolve any remaining sugar. Beat in the eggs.

4. Microwave on HIGH for 2 minutes, then on MEDIUM for 6 minutes, stirring every minute.

5. Pour into clean warm jars and cover each with a circle of greaseproof paper and a lid.

6. Keep in a cool place and eat within 3 weeks.

STRAWBERRY JAM WITH COINTREAU

MAKES ABOUT 675 g (1½ lb)

•

450 g (1 lb) frozen strawberries

30 ml (2 tbsp) lemon juice

450 g (1 lb) white granulated sugar

5 ml (1 tsp) butter

30 ml (2 tbsp) Cointreau

Preserving, using the microwave, is much easier than using traditional methods. You can make small quantities; the fruit stays whole and of course it is much quicker. Strawberry jam is best made with just-picked fruit so if you pick your own freeze them and make the jam up as needed. Jars can be sterilized in the microwave: put a little water in the base of each jar and microwave on HIGH until the water boils. Drain the jars and invert on paper towels until required. Store the jam in a cool dark place so the colour is retained.

1. Defrost strawberries in the microwave on LOW for 10–12 minutes. Drain the juice into a large glass mixing bowl (able to withstand high temperatures) and reserve the strawberries.

2. Microwave the sugar in the bag or in a bowl on HIGH for 4 minutes.

3. Stir the lemon juice into the strawberry juice and microwave on HIGH for 2 minutes or until boiling. Stir in the warmed sugar and microwave on HIGH for 6 minutes, stirring every 2 minutes or until the sugar is dissolved.

4. Add the strawberries and microwave on HIGH for 5 minutes.

5. Stir in the butter and microwave on HIGH for a further 5 minutes. Test for setting by putting a teaspoon of jam on to a cold plate: it should wrinkle when pushed. Cook a little longer if necessary.

6. When the setting point is reached (the jam may seem a little sloppy but will firm up on cooling) add the Cointreau. Pour into sterilized jars and cover in the usual way. When cool store in the refrigerator.

—— COOK'S TIP——

If you want to cheat, warm a good shop bought jam in the microwave and add the Cointreau to it. This trick also works with brandy and marmalade!

VEGETARIAN

THESE DAYS MOST of us want to try vegetarian meals or have vegetarian friends whom we would love to entertain – if we only knew what to serve! This menu fits the bill perfectly. The food is colourful and varied in texture. The peperonata served at room temperature with chilled Greek strained yogurt and wheaten soda farl, tastes and looks delicious. The walnut-stuffed aubergines provide protein and a crunchy texture. They are filling, so a selection of salads should be all that is necessary to accompany them. Throw your ideas of healthy eating to the wind for the dessert, which is pure indulgence.

PEPERONATA

SERVES 6
•
1 large Spanish onion, sliced

2 cloves garlic, crushed

45 ml (3 tbsp) olive oil

675 g (1½ lb) mixed red, green and yellow peppers, seeded

1 × 397 g (14 oz) can chopped tomatoes

2.5 ml (½ tsp) salt

freshly ground black pepper

Peperonata is a dish that can be served hot or cold, either as a vegetable or a starter. We particularly like it served cold as a starter with Greek strained yogurt – the colours contrast beautifully. It does freeze although is not quite so good as when made fresh. On defrosting it would be worth draining and reducing the liquid a little before serving. At certain times during the year peppers are cheap so make the most of them then.

1. Combine the onion, garlic and oil in a large bowl and microwave on HIGH for 3 minutes.

2. Cut the peppers into 5 mm (¼ in) slices, add to the onion mixture and cover. Microwave on HIGH for 5 minutes.

3. Stir in the tomatoes, cover and microwave on HIGH for 5 minutes.

4. Uncover the bowl and microwave on HIGH for 20 minutes, stirring once or twice. The mixture should be fairly thick, and most of the liquid should have evaporated.

5. Season with the salt and pepper and serve immediately or cool and chill in the refrigerator until required.

WHEATEN SODA FARL

SERVES 6

•

225 g (8 oz) plain wholemeal flour

225 g (8 oz) plain flour

5 ml (1 tsp) bicarbonate of soda

15 ml (1 tbsp) baking powder

75 g (3 oz) soft margarine

300 ml (½ pt) milk

 This is a traditional Irish recipe, much loved. It is best served warm but is wonderful toasted if you have any left over. It freezes well.

1. Sift the flours, bicarbonate of soda and baking powder together into a bowl; do not discard the bran in the sieve but tip it back into the bowl.

2. Rub in the fat until the mixture resembles fine breadcrumbs.

3. Lightly stir in the milk but do not overmix. Knead gently (about 6–8 times) and shape into a round.

4. Place on a greased baking sheet suitable for your oven and cut the round into six, moving the pieces apart slightly (5 mm/¼ in) so there is room for them to expand.

5. Bake in a preheated combination oven at 180°C with LOW power microwave for 20 minutes. Cool on a wire rack.

AUBERGINES STUFFED WITH WALNUTS

SERVES 6

•

140 g (4½ oz) bulgur wheat

3 medium-sized aubergines

90 ml (6 tbsp) olive oil

1 large onion, finely chopped

2–3 cloves garlic, crushed

350 g (12 oz) tomatoes, skinned, seeded and roughly chopped

45 ml (3 tbsp) fresh parsley, chopped

175 g (6 oz) walnuts, roughly chopped

175 g (6 oz) Cheddar cheese, grated

salt and freshly ground black pepper

Interesting tasty vegetarian dishes that appeal to non-vegetarians are often hard to find. This is perfect, with its lovely full flavour and crunchy texture. The dish may be made completely in advance and reheated before serving, either in a hot oven or under the grill, so that the crunchy texture is retained.

1. Place the bulgur wheat in a bowl. Add cold water to cover and leave to soak for 30 minutes. Strain, squeezing out as much water as possible, and reserve.

2. Wipe the aubergines and score round the centre lengthways. Microwave on HIGH for 9–10 minutes or until soft.

3. Cut the aubergines in half lengthways and carefully scoop out the flesh. Chop the flesh, reserve the skins.

4. Combine the olive oil, onion and garlic in a dish and microwave on HIGH for 4 minutes stirring once.

5. Stir in the tomatoes, chopped aubergine, bulgur and all the other ingredients, seasoning to taste.

6. Stuff the aubergine skins with the mixture and place in a large greased shallow dish. Cook in a preheated combination oven at 220°C with LOW power microwave for 25 minutes.

BANOFFY PIE

SERVES 6
•
75 g (3 oz) butter

75 g (3 oz) semolina

50 g (2 oz) caster sugar

75 g (3 oz) plain flour

5 ml (1 tsp) cinnamon

Filling

75 g (3 oz) soft dark brown sugar

1 large egg

150 ml (5 fl oz) single cream

Topping

3 bananas

200 ml (7 fl oz) double cream

30 ml (2 tbsp) milk

5 ml (1 tsp) vanilla essence

10 ml (2 tsp) caster sugar

The name for this pie comes from the combination of bananas and toffee. We have had this pie in various restaurants throughout Northern Ireland and England but have never found a recipe for it, so with a willing crew of guinea pigs we set about making one up. It is extremely rich and calorific but worth every inch! If you wish to buy one sort of cream use 300 ml (10 fl oz) double cream for the topping and the filling, making the filling with 120 ml (4 fl oz) cream and a little milk. Make this on the day of serving, allowing time for it to cool. Slice the bananas and decorate just before serving.

1. Microwave the butter in a bowl on HIGH for 1 minute or until melted; stir in the semolina and sugar. Sift the flour and cinnamon together and mix well into the butter mixture, then press into the base of a 23 cm (9 in) flan dish or ring. Set aside.

2. Make the filling: place the brown sugar in a bowl and beat in the egg and cream.

3. Pour the filling into the flan case, and bake in a preheated combination oven at 180°C with LOW power microwave for 12–14 minutes or until the filling has just set. Set the flan aside to cool.

4. Just before serving make the topping: slice the bananas thinly and pile them on to the flan. Beat the cream with the milk, vanilla and caster sugar until it stands in soft peaks and cover the bananas so that neither the toffee custard nor the bananas can be seen. Serve at once.

MIDWEEK SPECIAL

SMOKED HADDOCK PÂTÉ

CHICKEN ITALIENNE

POTATOES WITH GARLIC AND PARSLEY

PEAS IN THE FRENCH WAY

POIRES AU GRENADINE

*T*HERE ARE TIMES when our ideas are grander than our bank account. This is a menu for just such an occasion. We have chosen food that looks and tastes good but that does not cost too much to make. The smoked haddock pâté starter, when placed in individual ramekins and garnished, looks lovely and is filling when served with crusty brown bread. Chicken Italienne makes good use of those inexpensive and underused poultry portions – chicken thighs. If you buy them frozen you may find that they need to be trimmed (in fact you can often get another meal from the trimmings). If possible buy them fresh; most big supermarkets sell them in packets of 8.

The dessert of stuffed pears looks beautiful, with its glowing jewel colour. This is thanks to the grenadine, which can easily be bought from the off-licence. It is cheaper than a bottle of wine, will keep and has many other uses, for example in ice cream toppings and cocktails.

SMOKED HADDOCK PÂTÉ

SERVES 4–6
•
450 g (1 lb) smoked haddock

30 ml (2 tbsp) milk

75 g (3 oz) butter

125 g (4 oz) curd or cream cheese

15 ml (1 tbsp) lemon juice

salt and freshly ground black pepper

To Garnish

lemon slices

fresh parsley

Even if your guests are not great fish eaters, you can guarantee they will love this delicious starter. It is a delight for the hostess too as it is so quick to prepare and can even be made the day before. Serve it with chunks of wholemeal bread for a homely effect or with Melba toast (see page 30) for a more formal occasion.

1. Skin the haddock and place in a dish with the milk. Cover and microwave on HIGH for 6 minutes.

2. Drain the fish, flake and transfer to a bowl.

3. Beat in the butter, then work in the remaining ingredients. Spoon the pâté into a dish or use individual ramekins. Chill, then serve garnished with lemon and parsley.

—— COOK'S TIP ——

A little melted butter may be poured over the top of each ramekin and left to set. This helps to keep the pâté moist and seals in the flavour.

CHICKEN ITALIENNE

SERVES 4

•

15 ml (1 tbsp) olive oil

2 shallots, finely chopped

1 clove garlic, finely chopped

8 chicken thighs

8 thin slices of salami

1 stick celery, cut into matchsticks

150 ml (5 fl oz) white wine

150 ml (5 fl oz) chicken stock
(½ chicken stock cube will do)

½ small red pepper, seeded and
cut into small diamonds

½ small green pepper, seeded and
cut into small diamonds

25 g (1 oz) butter

25 g (1 oz) plain flour

45 ml (3 tbsp) double cream

An attractive economical recipe is useful in any cook's repertoire, and one that is also quick and easy must be doubly so. This fills the position beautifully. If you are feeling very broke, omit the wine and double up on the stock – it will still be delicious. There is plenty of sauce so it would go very well with green noodles instead of the potatoes with garlic and parsley.

Make this in advance up to the end of step 5, and finish it just before serving.

1. Combine the oil, shallots and garlic in a casserole dish large enough to accommodate all the chicken in a single layer. Microwave on HIGH for 3 minutes stirring once.

2. Meanwhile skin and bone the chicken thighs. Place them between 2 sheets of greaseproof paper or cling film and flatten them with a rolling pin.

3. Place a slice of salami and a few celery matchsticks on each thigh, roll up and secure with a cocktail stick.

4. Place the chicken on top of the onions in the casserole. Microwave on HIGH for 3 minutes.

5. Turn the chicken over, pour over the wine and stock, cover and microwave on HIGH for 6 minutes. Rearrange the chicken, add the red and green pepper and microwave on HIGH for 6 minutes more.

6. With a slotted spoon remove the chicken, onions and pepper and keep warm. Cream the butter and flour together and add gradually to the hot liquid, stirring constantly using a wire whisk.

7. Microwave the sauce on HIGH for 3 minutes or until boiling, stirring after each minute. Return the pepper and onion to the sauce and stir in the cream; keep warm without boiling.

8. Remove the cocktail sticks from the chicken and slice diagonally with a sharp knife so that you have circles exposing the filling. Arrange on a warm serving plate, pour over the sauce and serve.

POTATOES WITH GARLIC AND PARSLEY

SERVES 4
•
4 medium-sized potatoes, scrubbed but not peeled

2 cloves garlic, crushed

75 g (3 oz) butter

30 ml (2 tbsp) fresh parsley, chopped

salt and freshly ground black pepper

 This hearty dish started off its life being called peasant potatoes but this used to conjure up such funny pictures that we had to change the name – this one is much safer! Prepare this dish in advance. If you microwave it for a couple of minutes so that the butter spreads into every crack you should find that the potatoes will not discolour.

1. Cut the potatoes in half lengthways. Slash the cut side of each in a criss-cross pattern, taking care not to cut all the way through to the skin, otherwise the potatoes will fall apart.

2. Cream all the other ingredients together and push into the slits you have made.

3. Arrange in a shallow dish and cook in a preheated combination oven at 220°C with LOW power microwave for 20–25 minutes or until tender.

PEAS IN THE FRENCH WAY

SERVES 4–6
•
125 g (4 oz) Chinese leaves (the heart is the best part)

450 g (1 lb) frozen peas, defrosted

2 large carrots, peeled and cut into thin matchsticks

6 spring onions, chopped

10 ml (2 tsp) sugar

15 ml (1 tbsp) chopped fresh parsley

50 g (2 oz) butter

30 ml (2 tbsp) water

a pinch of salt

 This is an ideal vegetable dish for a dinner party as it can be prepared in advance and left unattended in the oven. Cooking time is also not too critical, so it will hold quite well before serving. A small round lettuce can be used in place of the Chinese leaves.

1. Shred the Chinese leaves and put them in the base of a medium-sized casserole.

2. Add all the remaining ingredients, cover and cook in a preheated combination oven at 180°C with LOW power microwave for about 20 minutes or until the carrot is tender.

—— COOK'S TIP——

Try adding a slice of cheese to turn this tasty potato dish into a complete meal.

POIRES AU GRENADINE

SERVES 4

•

25 g (1 oz) boudoir biscuits, crushed

25 g (1 oz) ground almonds

a pinch of ground cloves

45 ml (3 tbsp) lemon juice

4 firm Comice pears (or other short fat pears)

90 ml (6 tbsp) grenadine

5 ml (1 tsp) arrowroot

15 ml (1 tbsp) water

The beautiful pink colour of this dessert is to our minds far superior to that of pears cooked the traditional way in red wine. If you are feeling creative decorate the pears with a couple of chocolate rose or pear leaves (see Cook's tip). This is best served when it has cooled but if you wish to make it in advance keep the pears in the sauce without thickening it. Thicken the sauce shortly before serving, pouring it over the cool pears to serve.

1. Mix the crushed biscuits, almonds and cloves together in a bowl and stir in half the lemon juice.

2. Peel the pears, leaving the stalks on. Slice a small piece from the base of each so that they stand upright.

3. Cut the top off each pear and hollow out the centres; pack with the almond mixture and replace the tops.

4. Stand the pears in a deep dish and pour the remaining lemon juice and grenadine over. Cover and microwave on HIGH for 4 minutes.

5. Baste well and test with a skewer. If not tender microwave on HIGH for 2 minutes more or until ready.

6. With a slotted spoon, remove the pears and arrange on individual serving plates. Mix the arrowroot with the water and add to the pear liquid. Microwave on HIGH for 2 minutes or until clear. Pour the sauce over the pears and serve.

—— COOK'S TIP——

To make chocolate leaves, wash and dry rose or pear leaves. Dip the undersides in melted chocolate (or brush this on, if preferred). When the chocolate is set, peel off the leaves.

ROMANTIC DINNER FOR 2

HIGHLAND AVOCADO

PORK FILLET WITH CRANBERRY AND GINGER SAUCE

CASSEROLED BABY NEW POTATOES

RIBBONED COURGETTES

BLACK AND WHITE CHOCOLATE MOUSSE

*T*HERE ARE OCCASIONS when you really want to spoil yourself and your partner – celebrating anniversaries, birthdays or even just being together. Of course you could go out for dinner, but what could be more romantic than eating by candlelight in your own home. You do not have to argue over who is going to drive either!

Prepare everything in advance, dress for the occasion and have a bottle of champagne on ice. All that remains is to turn the lights down low, put some music and make an occasion!

HIGHLAND AVOCADO

SERVES 2
•
2 unsmoked streaky bacon rashers, rind removed

50 g (2 oz) button mushrooms, wiped and finely sliced

25 g (1 oz) finely chopped onion

1 avocado

10 ml (2 tsp) lemon juice

25 g (1 oz) Cheddar cheese, grated

10 ml (2 tsp) mayonnaise

salt and freshly ground black pepper

 This is a delicious and unusual way of serving avocado. It can be made an hour or so in advance. If you coat the avocado well it should not spoil but do not do step 5 until just before you wish to serve them.

1. Cut the bacon into small pieces, put in a bowl and microwave on HIGH for 1 minute.

2. Add the mushrooms and chopped onion, stir and microwave on HIGH for 3 minutes.

3. Cut the avocado in half. Carefully scoop out the flesh, keeping the shells whole. Slice the flesh thinly and mix with the lemon juice.

4. Add all the other ingredients, season and pile back into the avocado shells.

5. Microwave the filled avocado halves for 2½ minutes on HIGH before serving on individual plates garnished with a little lettuce.

PORK FILLET WITH CRANBERRY AND GINGER SAUCE

SERVES 2
•
1 pork fillet

15 ml (1 tbsp) cranberry sauce

grated rind and juice of ½ orange

5 ml (1 tsp) ground ginger

5 ml (1 tsp) brown sugar

red wine (see method)

2.5 ml (½ tsp) arrowroot

10 ml (2 tsp) water

orange slices to garnish

 One pork fillet is an ideal quantity to serve 2 and as this recipe is simple and looks so attractive, we thought it was an ideal dish for a romantic dinner.

1. Wipe the fillet and remove any loose fat. Lay in a shallow dish.

2. Combine the cranberry sauce, orange rind and juice, ginger and sugar in a blender or food processor and blend until smooth.

3. Brush the pork with a little of the sauce and roast in a preheated combination oven at 220°C with LOW power microwave for 12–14 minutes. Remove the pork, cover and leave to stand while making the sauce.

4. Drain the cranberry mixture into a measuring jug and make up to 120 ml (4 fl oz) with wine. Microwave on HIGH for 2 minutes. Blend the arrowroot with the water in a cup, then stir into the sauce and reheat on HIGH for 1 minute or until clear.

5. Slice the pork thinly and arrange on dinner plates. Coat with sauce and serve, garnished with orange slices.

BABY NEW POTATOES

SERVES 2
•
350 g (12 oz) baby new potatoes

25 g (1 oz) butter

1 sprig each of thyme, parsley and rosemary

salt and freshly ground black pepper

1. Scrub the potatoes but do not peel them, and place them in a small casserole with all the other ingredients.

2. Bake in a preheated oven at 200°C with LOW power microwave for 20 minutes or until tender.

OPPOSITE
Romantic dinner for two (pages 139–145); Highland avocado; Pork fillet with cranberry and ginger sauce served with Casseroled baby new potatoes and Ribboned courgettes; Black and white chocolate mousse.

OVERLEAF
Petit fours (pages 118–120); From left to right: Fresh cream truffles; Collettes; Peppermint creams; Fudge and Coconut ice.

RIBBONED COURGETTES

SERVES 2

•

225 g (8 oz) small courgettes

15 g (½ oz) butter

5 ml (1 tsp) snipped fresh chives

salt and freshly ground black pepper

1 or 2 chive flowers for decoration

 Courgettes prepared in this way look very pretty, especially when garnished with chive flowers, and for best results they need to be cooked at the last minute.

1. Using a potato peeler cut the courgettes lengthways into thin slices. Discard the first and last slice which will be all skin; you should be left with long thin ribbons.

2. Place the courgettes in a dish with the butter and chives, cover and microwave on HIGH for 3–4 minutes, stirring once. Season to taste and serve immediately, garnished with the chive flowers.

BLACK AND WHITE CHOCOLATE MOUSSE

SERVES 2

•

125 g (4 oz) white chocolate

25 g (1 oz) unsalted butter

15 ml (1 tsp) Cointreau

90 ml (6 tbsp) double cream, softly whipped

1 egg white

75 g (3 oz) plain chocolate

1. Put 75 g (3 oz) of the white chocolate into a bowl, microwave on MEDIUM for 2–4 minutes or until melted, watching carefully.

2. Stir the butter into the chocolate with the liqueur. Microwave for 1 minute more on HIGH.

3. Beat the egg white until stiff and add to the chocolate with the cream. Fold carefully and divide the mixture between 2 chocolate pots. Chill the mousse for 2–3 hours, until set.

4. Microwave the plain chocolate on HIGH for 1–2 minutes until melted. Spread a little on to non-stick paper on which you have drawn a few small hearts, or use a small heart-shaped cutter when the chocolate is almost set. Spread the remaining plain chocolate on top of the mousse.

5. Microwave the remaining 25 g (1 oz) of white chocolate on HIGH for about 45 seconds until melted and make some small hearts in the same way as before. Decorate the mousse with the dark and light chocolate hearts.

PREVIOUS PAGE
Afternoon tea (pages 146–149); From left to right: Caraway scones; Vanilla slice; Chocolate fruit and nut squares and Orange drizzle shortbread; Date and Walnut layer cake; Cucumber sandwiches; Djaarjeeling tea.

OPPOSITE
Chinese menu à la carte (pages 125–128); From left to right: Chao Shao with bean sprouts; Spare ribs; Chinese beef with peppers, mushrooms and cashew nuts; Rice; Mange tout with water chestnuts; Lychees.

AFTERNOON TEA

AFTERNOON TEA IS becoming fashionable again. After years of baked beans on toast, dainty sandwiches, scones and scrumptious cakes are all the rage. Tea shops are appearing on the high street again and even tea dances are being revived. We give you a selection of biscuits and cakes which may be accompanied by small cucumber, pâté or egg sandwiches. Give the birds a treat and cut the crusts off, then serve the sandwiches garnished with cress.

Dig out all your best china, lace tablecloths and freshly laundered napkins or, if this is too much, just splash out on a packet of doylies.

Experiment by serving one of the many traditional teas, such as Earl Grey, Darjeeling or Lapsang Souchong.

CARAWAY SCONES

MAKES ABOUT 16
•
125 g (4 oz) self-raising flour

125 g (4 oz) wholemeal
self-raising flour

50 g (2 oz) butter

15 ml (1 tbsp) black treacle

1 egg

milk (see method)

caraway, poppy or sesame seeds

Scones are always a favourite at teatime, but these are extra-special. Wholemeal scones always seem to be heavy, but by using a mixture of flours in this recipe we get the best of both worlds. Caraway seeds give an unusual flavour, but we sometimes use poppy or sesame seeds too. A mixture of different toppings makes an attractive, wholesome-looking display.

1. Mix the flours together in a bowl, then rub in the butter until the mixture resembles fine breadcrumbs.

2. Add the black treacle. Beat the egg lightly in a measuring jug and make up to 150 ml (5 fl oz) with milk.

3. Stir into the flour with a fork, then knead lightly to form a soft dough. If too wet, add a little extra flour.

4. Roll out on a floured surface to 1 cm (½ in) thick. Cut into rounds using a 6 cm (2½ in) cutter.

5. Place the scones on a greased baking dish, brush with milk and sprinkle with caraway seeds. Bake in a preheated combination oven, using only conventional heat, at 200°C for 10 minutes or until well risen and golden brown. Serve with fresh strawberry jam (see page 131) and whipped cream.

CHOCOLATE FRUIT AND NUT SQUARES

MAKES ABOUT 24 SLICES
•
125 g (4 oz) unsalted butter

125 g (4 oz) caster sugar

30 ml (2 tbsp) cocoa powder

5 ml (1 tsp) vanilla essence

1 egg, lightly beaten

75 g (3 oz) desiccated coconut

75 g (3 oz) walnuts, chopped

75 g (3 oz) glacé cherries, quartered

225 g (8 oz) digestive biscuits, crushed

175 g (6 oz) plain chocolate, broken into squares

A very quick refrigerator slice, which can have endless variations by using different fruits and nuts. It is popular with both children and adults and if it is not all eaten at once, will keep well in an airtight tin for a week.

1. Combine the butter, sugar and cocoa powder in a large glass bowl and microwave on HIGH for 3 minutes.

2. Stir in the vanilla and beaten egg and microwave on HIGH for 1 minute.

3. Stir in the coconut, walnuts, cherries and crushed biscuits. Mix well and press into a greased and base-lined 20 × 25 cm (8 × 10 in) dish. Chill in the refrigerator.

4. When the base is firm, place the chocolate in a small bowl and microwave on HIGH for 4 minutes. Stir well until melted, microwaving for a little longer, if necessary. (This will depend on the type of chocolate used.)

5. Spread the chocolate over the base and chill again. Cut into small squares and serve for tea or as an after-dinner sweet.

ORANGE DRIZZLE SHORTBREAD

MAKES 16–24 PIECES
•
350 (12 oz) plain flour

125 g (4 oz) caster sugar

225 g (8 oz) butter, cubed

grated rind and juice of 1 orange

125 g (4 oz) icing sugar

If you make this interesting variation in a mixer or food processor it will be even easier then traditional shortbread because you don't even have to get your hands dirty! This freezes well both cooked and uncooked; in fact, we keep a bag of the mixture in the freezer ready to be shaken into a dish to cook for hungry children and unexpected guests!

1. Sift the flour and sugar into a mixing bowl. Rub in the butter until the mixture resembles breadcrumbs.

2. Stir in the grated orange rind and 30 ml (2 tbsp) of the orange juice.

3. Sprinkle the mixture into two 18 cm (7 in) sandwich dishes or tins (if permitted in your oven).

4. Bake in a preheated combination oven at 200°C with LOW power micro-wave for 12–14 minutes.

5. Meanwhile cream the icing sugar with a little of the remaining orange juice to make a glacé icing. Drizzle this over the shortbread whilst it is still warm, and cut into slices.

6. Remove from the tin and finish cooling on a rack.

DATE AND WALNUT LAYER CAKE

SERVES 8
•
125 g (4 oz) plain flour

10 ml (2 tsp) baking powder

5 ml (1 tbsp) mixed spice

75 g (3 oz) soft margarine

125 g (4 oz) caster sugar

125 g (4 oz) semolina

2 eggs, lightly beaten

60 ml (4 tbsp) milk

Crumble

75 g (3 oz) butter

75 g (3 oz) demerara sugar

50 g (2 oz) walnuts, roughly chopped

50 g (2 oz) dates, chopped

50 g (2 oz) plain flour

50 g (2 oz) semolina

15 ml (1 tbsp) cinnamon

 This teatime cake has proved popular with our friends. When it is sliced, there is quite a surprise because the interior has a marbled appearance. This cake has the added advantage of freezing well.

1. Sift the flour, baking powder and spice together and rub in the soft margarine.

2. Stir in the sugar, semolina, beaten eggs and milk. Set aside.

3. Make the crumble: microwave the butter on HIGH for 1 minute, then stir in all the other ingredients.

4. Grease and base-line a 20 cm (8 in) cake dish or tin suitable for your oven. Put a third of the cake mixture into the dish, top with a third of the crumble mixture and repeat until all the mixture is used up, finishing with the crumble mixture.

5. Bake in a preheated combination oven at 200°C with LOW power micro-wave for 16–20 minutes or until the cake feels firm and a skewer inserted in the centre comes out clean. Cool for 10 minutes in the dish before removing.

VANILLA SLICE

SERVES 6–8

•

225 g (½ lb) puff pastry

25 g (1 oz) butter

50 g (2 oz) icing sugar

15 ml (1 tbsp) sieved raspberry jam

Confectioners' Custard

300 ml (½ pt) milk

30 ml (2 tbsp) cornflour

25 g (1 oz) caster sugar

1 egg

2.5 ml (½ tsp) vanilla essence

This is an impressive looking, but surprisingly simple teatime treat. The trick of rolling the extra butter into the pastry makes the slice particularly light. The same idea can be used for a Mille Feuille to serve as a dessert. "Mille Feuille" means "1000 leaves", presumably the number of layers one should have in the pastry. We are not sure that our pastry has that number of leaves but it is certainly light! For a Mille Feuille, slice the pastry into 3 and fill with whipped cream and strawberries. Dust with icing sugar.

1. Roll out the pastry to a rectangle, spread with the butter, fold over and seal the edges with a rolling pin.

2. Roll out the pastry to a rectangle, about 10 × 30 cm (4 × 12 in). Trim the edges.

3. Place on a baking dish and cook in a preheated combination oven at 220°C, using conventional heat only, for about 10 minutes or until well risen and golden brown. Leave to cool.

4. To make the custard, blend a little of the milk with the cornflour in a cup. Mix the remaining milk, sugar and egg in a bowl, add the cornflour mixture and whisk well. Microwave on HIGH for 2 minutes, whisk thoroughly, then microwave on HIGH for 1½ minutes more, whisking every 30 seconds. Whisk in the vanilla essence. Leave to cool, covered with damp greaseproof paper.

5. When both pastry and custard are cold, assemble the vanilla slice: split the pastry in half and fill with custard. Replace the lid.

6. Sift the icing sugar into a bowl and add a little water. Stir to make a glacé icing. Coat the top of the slice. Pipe lines across the slice with the sieved jam, then drag a skewer across first in one direction, then in the other to form feather icing.

7. When the icing has set, cut into slices and serve.

CHRISTMAS DINNER

CHRISTMAS DINNER IS often the biggest meal of the year. People spend weeks planning and shopping for it, and then on the day itself, having got up at the crack of dawn to start the turkey off, they are often too tired to enjoy it all. These days many of us have had several roast turkey and Christmas pudding dinners by the time December 25th dawns so here is an alternative menu to refresh the palate.

If you prefer to cook a completely traditional meal, the turkey may be quickly cooked and the Christmas pudding reheated in minutes with the aid of your combination oven. Do not feel you have to cook absolutely everything in your combination oven; use it in conjunction with your other appliances to make the whole meal run smoothly.

ROAST GOOSE WITH TWO STUFFINGS

SERVES UP TO 10 WHEN STUFFED
•
6 kg (12–14 lb) oven-ready goose

salt (see method)

Goose makes a change from roast turkey at Christmas. It is a strongly flavoured meat and needs well-flavoured stuffings (see page 151). There is not as much meat on a goose as on a turkey so it will feed fewer guests. You are unlikely to have a lot left over, but if there is a little it is lovely in a cassoulet. Don't throw away the fat. It is very good for frying potatoes. Traditionally goose grease was applied to sprains; often the mere glimpse of the jar was enough to effect a recovery!

1. Remove all the fat from the inside of the goose.

2. Prick the bird all over with a fork, then rub with salt.

3. Fill with the stuffings (opposite) or of your own choice and secure. Weigh the stuffed goose, then place upside down on a rack above a roasting pan. Cover with a sheet of greaseproof paper.

4. Cook in a preheated combination oven at 200°C with LOW power micro-wave for 9 minutes per 450 g (1 lb) turning halfway through. The greaseproof paper should be removed 30 minutes before the end of the cooking time.

5. A lot of fat will come from the bird and is is important that this be drained

off at intervals during the cooking time, or it will attract microwave energy and slow down the cooking process.

6. Use the juices that are released during the final 30 minutes of cooking to make the gravy.

SAUSAGE, CELERY AND APPLE STUFFING

15 ml (1 tbsp) oil
1 onion, finely chopped
4 sticks celery, finely sliced
1 large cooking apple, peeled, cored and chopped
450 g (1 lb) sausage meat
125 g (4 oz) fresh bread-crumbs
1 egg
salt and freshly ground black pepper

 The two stuffing recipes we have given here compliment the goose well, so use either or better still both of them for a lovely meal. The stuffings will help to extend the goose to feed 10 generously.

1. Combine the oil, onion and celery in a bowl and microwave on HIGH power for 4 minutes.

2. Cool and mix with all the remaining ingredients. Stir well and use to stuff the goose.

PRUNE AND ORANGE STUFFING

175 g (6 oz) prunes, stoned and roughly chopped
150 ml (5 fl oz) fresh orange juice
15 ml (1 tbsp) oil
1 onion, finely chopped
grated rind of 1 orange
125 g (4 oz) coarse oatmeal, toasted
125 g (4 oz) breadcrumbs
1 egg
salt and freshly ground black pepper

1. Soak the prunes in the orange juice for several hours or overnight.

2. Combine the oil and the onion in a bowl and microwave on HIGH power for 3 minutes. Add the prunes and stir in all the remaining ingredients.

3. Season to taste and use to stuff the goose.

BRUSSELS SPROUTS WITH CHESTNUTS

SERVES 4
•
450 g (1 lb) Brussels sprouts

125 g (4 oz) frozen chestnuts

salt

butter

Sprouts can be a bit tricky to cook in the microwave, but we find that if we use even-sized ones, about the size of a walnut, and cut a slit in each stem, they cook very well. Another tip is to slice the sprouts from top to stalk, cutting each one into 3. Rinse the slices in water, add a knob of butter and cook quickly, like cabbage. In this recipe, the combination of sprouts and chestnuts is delicious and goes particularly well with turkey or game dishes.

1. Trim the sprouts and cut a slit in each stalk. Place the frozen sprouts and chestnuts in a casserole and barely cover with water.

2. Add a pinch of salt, cover the dish and microwave on HIGH for 10 minutes.

3. Drain and toss in butter before serving.

CARROT STICKS WITH LEMON AND CARDOMOM

SERVES 4
•
450 g (1 lb) carrots

5 cm (2 in) length of lemon rind

6 whole cardomom pods

50 g (2 oz) butter

5 ml (1 tsp) sugar

15 ml (1 tbsp) water

salt and freshly ground black pepper

This has a lovely fresh bright colour, tastes delicious and is a wonderful accompaniment to lots of different dishes. In the summer, when new carrots are available, try using them whole; adjusting the cooking time accordingly. This dish can be made in advance and reheated without spoiling the appearance or flavour. If this is done it is a good idea to undercook the carrots, something which makes good sense in terms of nutrition. A final word of warning: if you make this in advance be sure to make plenty, or hide it as it is so delicious it has a habit of disappearing.

1. Scrub or peel the carrots and cut into 4 × 1 cm × 5 mm (1½ × ½ × ¼ in) sticks.

2. Cut the lemon rind into very fine julienne. Using a garlic press, crush the cardomom pods so they split slightly.

3. Combine all the ingredients except the salt and pepper in a dish. Cover and microwave on HIGH for 7–10 minutes or until just tender, stirring once or twice.

4. Season to taste – you will not need very much salt.

FROZEN GINGER MERINGUE PUDDING

SERVES 6

•

300 ml (½ pt) whipping cream

125 g (4 oz) crystallised ginger, very finely chopped

125 g (4 oz) meringues, lightly crushed

To Decorate

crystallised ginger

melted chocolate

This sweet couldn't be simpler to prepare, but always earns approval with its contrast of cream and crisp meringue. It makes a delightful alternative to the more traditional Christmas pudding. If you want to really make it festive, make some chocolate holly leaves to decorate it (see Cook's tip page 126).

1. Whip the cream to soft peaks. Stir in the ginger.

2. Gently mix in the meringues and carefully pack into 1 litre (1¾ pt) pudding basin. Freeze.

3. To unmould the pudding, dip it into a bowl of hot water for about 30 seconds to melt the edge, put a serving plate on top and invert the mould – it should drop out; if not, warm it a little more. Return to the freezer while you melt the chocolate, decorate with drizzled chocolate and a little chopped ginger.

4. Store in the freezer, but transfer to the refrigerator about 20 minutes before serving to soften the pudding.

MINCEMEAT HANDKERCHIEFS

MAKES 12

•

3 sheets of filo pastry

75 g (3 oz) butter, melted

225 g (8 oz) fruit mincemeat

150 ml (5 fl oz) double cream, lightly whipped

These make a change from the traditional mince pie. The cases can be made 24 hours in advance, but be careful how you store them as they are delicate. Try filling them with jam or fresh fruit and cream for an impressive quick dessert.

1. Grease a 12-hole bun tin.

2. Cut the filo pastry into 10 cm (4 in) squares, brush with the butter and arrange 3 squares in each bun tin. Offset the points of the squares so that they resemble handkerchief points.

3. Bake in a preheated combination oven at 220°C, using conventional heat only, for about 7 minutes or until golden, watching carefully because they will burn very quickly.

4. Cool on a wire rack, then fill with a little mincemeat and cream.

USEFUL CHARTS

The following charts are an at-a-glance guide to defrosting and cooking ingredients in the oven using either your microwave or microwave/combination facility. For more detailed timings refer to your manufacturer's handbook.

MICROWAVING PASTA AND RICE

PASTA/RICE	QUANTITY	PREPARATION	COOKING TIME ON HIGH POWER	TIPS
AMERICAN LONG GRAIN OR PATNA RICE	225 g (8 oz)	Place in deep covered dish with knob of butter. Cover with 600 ml (1 pt) boiling water, salted	12–14 mins. Stand for 5 mins	Stir halfway
BROWN RICE	125 g (4 oz)	600 ml (1 pt) boiling water, salted	30 mins	Stir halfway, drain
LASAGNE	225 g (8 oz)	Add 1 litre (1¾ pt) boiling salted water and 15 ml (1 tbsp) oil	10 mins. Stand for 2 mins	Cook uncovered. Stir halfway
MACARONI AND SMALL PASTA NOODLES	225 g (8 oz)	Place in deep dish with 15 ml (1 tbsp) oil and cover with 750 ml (1¼ pt) boiling salted water	8 mins. Stand for 3 mins	Cook uncovered. Stir halfway
SPAGHETTI	225 g (8 oz)	Break in half and place in a dish. Cover with 750 ml (1¼ pt) boiling salted water	10 mins. Stand for 2 mins	Cook uncovered. Stir halfway

MICROWAVING FRESH FRUIT

FRUIT	QUANTITY	PREPARATION	COOKING TIME ON HIGH POWER
APPLES (eg, BRAMLEYS)	450 g (1 lb)	Peel, core and slice. Sprinkle with sugar to taste	6–8 mins
APRICOTS	450 g (1 lb)	Stone, wash, sprinkle with sugar to taste. Stir halfway	6–8 mins
BLACKCURRANTS, REDCURRANTS, LOGANBERRIES, BLACKBERRIES etc	450 g (1 lb)	Top and tail, wash and sprinkle with sugar to taste	3–5 mins

GOOSEBERRIES	450 g (1 lb)	Top and tail, wash and sprinkle with sugar to taste		4–5 mins
PEACHES	4 medium sized	Stone and wash – sprinkle with sugar		4–5 mins
PEARS	450 g (1 lb)	Peel, core and cut in half. Dissolve 50–75 g (2–3 oz) sugar in hot water and pour over pears		6–8 mins
PLUMS, CHERRIES, DAMSONS, GREENGAGES	450 g (1 lb)	Stone and wash. Sprinkle with sugar to taste		4–6 mins
RHUBARB	450 g (1 lb)	Wash, trim and cut into short pieces. Add approx 125 g (4 oz) sugar		7–10 mins

MICROWAVING FRESH VEGETABLES

VEGETABLE	QUANTITY	PREPARATION	SALTED WATER	COOKING TIME ON HIGH POWER
ASPARAGUS	450 g (1 lb)	Trim, leave whole	60 ml (4 tbsp)	6–8 mins
AUBERGINES	450 g (1 lb)	Wash, slice, sprinkle with salt. Leave for 30 mins. Rinse before cooking	30 ml (2 tbsp)	8–10 mins
BROAD BEANS	450 g (1 lb)	Remove them from pods	45 ml (3 tbsp)	6–8 mins
FRENCH BEANS	450 g (1 lb)	Wash and cut	30 ml (2 tbsp)	8–10 mins
RUNNER BEANS	450 g (1 lb)	String and slice	30 ml (2 tbsp)	8–10 mins
BEETROOT	450 g (1 lb)	Peel and slice	30 ml (2 tbsp)	8–10 mins
WHOLE BEETROOT	450 g (1 lb)	Scrub and pierce	30 ml (2 tbsp)	12–14 mins
BROCCOLI	450 g (1 lb)	Trim and cut into spears	30 ml (2 tbsp)	8–12 mins
BRUSSELS SPROUTS	450 g (1 lb)	Trim, remove outer leaves and wash	30 ml (2 tbsp)	8–10 mins
CABBAGE	450 g (1 lb)	Wash and shred leaves	30 ml (2 tbsp)	8–10 mins
CARROTS	450 g (1 lb)	New/small: wash, scrape, leave whole. Old: scrape and thinly slice	30 ml (2 tbsp) 30 ml (2 tbsp)	7–10 mins 7–10 mins
CAULIFLOWER	450 g (1 lb)	Cut into florets	60 ml (4 tbsp)	10–12 mins
CELERY	450 g (1 lb)	Wash, trim and slice	45 ml (3 tbsp)	7–10 mins
CORN ON THE COB	2 medium	Wrap each in grease-proof paper with knob of butter	—	6–8 mins
COURGETTES	450 g (1 lb)	Wash, trim and slice, add 25 g (1 oz) butter and cover	—	8–10 mins

LEEKS	450 g (1 lb)	Wash, trim and slice	30 ml (2 tbsp)	7–10 mins
MARROW	450 g (1 lb)	Peel, cut into rings 2 cm (¾ in) thick. Remove seeds and quarter rings	30 ml (2 tbsp)	8–10 mins
ONIONS	2 large	1. Peel and slice 2. Peel and chop	30 ml (2 tbsp) 30 ml (2 tbsp)	6–7 mins 4–5 mins
PARSNIPS	450 g (1 lb)	Peel and slice	30 ml (2 tbsp)	8–10 mins
PEAS	450 g (1 lb)	Remove from pods	30 ml (2 tbsp)	8–10 mins
POTATOES: NEW	450 g (1 lb)	Wash thoroughly but leave in skin	90 ml (6 tbsp)	6–8 mins
POTATOES: OLD	450 g (1 lb)	Wash and scrub thoroughly, dry and prick with a fork	—	8–10 mins
SPINACH	450 g (1 lb)	Wash, break up thick stalks	—	6–8 mins
SPRING GREENS	450 g (1 lb)	Wash, break up thick stalks and shred	30 ml (2 tbsp)	6–8 mins
SWEDE	450 g (1 lb)	Peel and dice	30 ml (2 tbsp)	7–8 mins
WHOLE SWEDE	450 g (1 lb)	Scrub and cut a slice from the base, turn halfway, stand 5 mins at end	300 ml (½ pt) hot	12–14 mins
TOMATOES	450 g (1 lb)	Wash and halve Cover	—	3–6 mins
TURNIPS	450 g (1 lb)	Peel and slice	30 ml (2 tbsp)	8–10 mins
WHOLE TURNIP	450 g (1 lb)	Scrub and cut a slice from the bottom, turn halfway, leave to stand 5 mins	300 ml (½ pt) hot	10–12 mins

DEFROSTING

Many combination ovens now have an automatic defrost programme which allows standing time between bursts of microwave energy, to give even defrosting of foods. If your combination oven does not have this facility, we find the best way of defrosting is to follow a similar procedure. For example, for a whole chicken, set 10 minutes on LOW power, rest for 10 minutes, then repeat until the chicken is defrosted.

All foods should be turned halfway through the defrosting time and mince etc. should be broken up with a fork.

If your combination oven has a fan this may be used (without conventional heat but with LOW power microwave) to speed up defrosting times.

DEFROSTING AND MICROWAVING FISH

FISH	QUANTITY	DEFROSTING TIME AT LOW POWER	COOKING TIME AT HIGH POWER
HERRING, TROUT AND MACKEREL	225 g (8 oz) fish gutted but whole	5 mins. Stand for 10–15 mins	4–6 mins
KIPPERS	450 g (1 lb) fillets	5 mins. Stand for 5–10 mins	3–5 mins
SALMON STEAKS	450 g (1 lb)	5 mins. Stand for 5 mins	4–5 mins
SHELL FISH: PRAWNS, SCAMPI	450 g (1 lb)	2 mins. Stand for 10 mins	Use as required
SMOKED FISH, HADDOCK OR COD	450 g (1 lb)	5 mins. Stand for 5 mins	4–5 mins
WHITE FISH – COD, HADDOCK, COLEY, PLAICE OR SOLE	450 g (1 lb) prepared fillets	5 mins. Stand for 5 mins	4–6 mins

COOKING MEAT OR POULTRY

MEAT OR POULTRY	TEMPERATURE	POWER LEVEL	TIME PER 450 g (1 lb)	TIPS
BEEF: RARE	220°C	Low	10 mins	
MEDIUM	200°C	Low	13 mins	
WELL DONE	180°C	Low	16 mins	
LAMB: MEDIUM	200°C	Low	18–20 mins	Leave to stand for 10–15 mins covered
WELL DONE	200°C	Low	20–22 mins	
PORK	200°C	Low		
GAMMON	See recipe			
CHICKEN	200°C	Low	12–15 mins	
DUCK	220°C	Medium	8–10 mins	
TURKEY	220°C	Low	8 mins	Turn halfway, leave for 10 mins then the juices should run clear
PHEASANT	See recipe			
PIGEON	See recipe			
OTHER GAME BIRDS	200°C	Low	9–10 mins	
PORTIONS OF MEAT				
CHICKEN QUARTERS (4)	200°C	Low	16–20 mins	
CHICKEN EIGHTHS (4)	200°C	Low	12–15 mins	
LAMB CHOPS (4)	200°C	Low	12–14 mins	
PORK CHOPS (4)	220°C	Low	12–14 mins	

INDEX

INDEX